W9-BYV-688

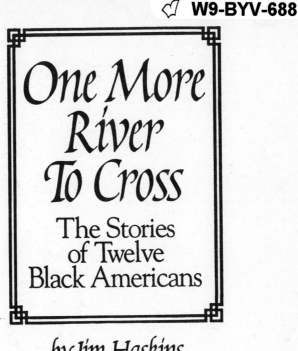

One More River To Cross

The Stories of Twelve Black Americans

by Jim Haskins

SCHOLASTIC INC.
New York Toronto London Auckland Sydney

Cover and Interior Photo Credits

Crispus Attucks courtesy of the Association for the Study of Negro Life and History, Inc. Madam C. J. Walker courtesy of the Indiana Historical Society Library (neg. no. C2140). Matthew Henson courtesy of Historical Pictures Service, Chicago. Marian Anderson courtesy of AP/Wide World. Ralph Bunche courtesy of the United Nations. Charles Drew courtesy of The American National Red Cross. Romare Bearden courtesy of the Museum of Art, Baltimore, MD. Fannie Lou Hamer courtesy of AP/Wide World. Eddie Robinson courtesy of Grambling State University. Shirley Chisholm courtesy of the Moorland-Spingarn Research Center, Howard University. Malcolm X courtesy of AP/Wide World. Ronald McNair courtesy of AP/Wide World.

If you purchased this book without a cover, you should be aware that this book is stolen property. It was reported as "unsold and destroyed" to the publisher, and neither the author nor the publisher has received any payment for this "stripped book."

No part of this publication may be reproduced in whole or in part, or stored in a retrieval system, or transmitted in any form, or by any means, electronic, mechanical, photocopying, recording, or otherwise, without written permission of the publisher. For information regarding permission, write to Scholastic Inc., 730 Broadway, New York, NY 10003.

ISBN 0-590-42897-7

Copyright © 1992 by James Haskins.
All rights reserved. Published by Scholastic Inc.

24 23 22 21 20 19 18 17 16 15 14 13   9/9 0/0

Printed in the U.S.A.   40

I am grateful to Kathy Benson, Patricia Allen-Brown, Ann Kalkhoff, Karen Picket, and Rachel Ray for their help.

FOR ESTHER HOUSTON-VASSAR
"making a difference"

Contents

Introduction

Since blacks first arrived in this country as slaves from Africa, thousands upon thousands have made major contributions to America. From music to science to law to business to politics, there are few if any areas of American and world life that have not been touched and made better by black Americans.

The twelve people in this book represent this wide range of influence. Crispus Attucks was the first American to die in the cause of independence. Ronald McNair was the first black American to die in the effort to control outer space. Matthew Henson was one of the first two human beings to reach the North Pole, and Dr. Charles R. Drew invented a technique that has saved thousands of human lives. Each man had to overcome the barriers of being black in a racist society to make his contributions.

Women like Madam C. J. Walker and Shirley Chisholm had to overcome not only the barriers of being black in a racist society but also the barriers of being a woman in a male-dominated society in order to become pioneers in the fields of business and politics.

Most of the twelve also had to surmount the additional barrier of poverty.

But all succeeded in spite of the obstacles put in their way. All possessed a sense of pride that made them feel they could overcome whatever barriers they met, and the courage to follow their dreams. And all have left or will leave behind a legacy of determination and excellence that will never be forgotten.

1
Crispus Attucks

Ran-away from his master *William Brown* of *Framingham*, on the 30th of Sept. last, a Molatto Fellow, about 27 Years of Age, named *Crispas*, 6 Feet two Inches high, short curl'd Hair, his Knees nearer together than common; had on a light colour'd Bearskin Coat, plain brown Fustian Jacket, or Brown all-Wool one, new Buckskin Breeches, blue YarnStockings, and a check'd woollenShirt.

Whoever shall take up said Runaway, and convey him to his abovesaid Master, shall have *ten Pounds*, old TenorReward, and all necessary Charges paid. And allMasters of Vessels and others, are hereby caution'd against concealing or carrying off saidServant on Penalty of the Law.

Boston Gazette, October 2, 1750

3

In 1770 Crispus Attucks, a black man born a slave, was the first American to die in the cause of the American Revolution. As the advertisement shows, he had already declared his own independence twenty years earlier.

Little is known about Crispus's early life. He was born into slavery, probably in the colony of Massachusetts. It is said that his father was African, and if so then his father was brought to the colonies on a slave ship. Crispus's mother was said to be an Indian and was probably a descendant of John Attucks.

John Attucks was a member of the Natick Indian tribe, and the word *attuck* in the language of the Naticks means deer. John Attucks lived in the 1600s and converted to Christianity. But during an Indian uprising that came to be known as King Philip's War, he sided with his own people. He was executed by New England colonists for treason in 1676.

Crispus was born some fifty years after that. We do not know anything about his upbringing, only that by 1750 he was a slave who belonged to a William Brown of Framingham.

According to local legend in Framingham, Attucks was an expert trader of horses and cattle, and dealt with free white men all the time. He kept the money he made for himself and probably tried to buy his freedom from William Brown. But Brown would not sell him his freedom, perhaps because Crispus was too valuable to him. So Crispus ran away.

In spite of the ad, Crispus was never caught and sent back to his master. No one knows what he did for the next twenty years. More than likely, he spent those years as a sailor, working on cargo ships that sailed to and from the West Indies, and on whaling ships off the New England coast.

During those same twenty years, trouble had arisen between England and her far-off colonies on the eastern coast of North America. Citizens of the colonies resented having to buy nearly everything they needed from England and complained about the lack of free trade. The colonies also complained of having to pay taxes to the king when they had no say in their own government.

Citizens of the colony of Massachusetts, especially in Boston, the capital of the colony, were the most outspoken in their complaints about British tyranny. So restive was that colony that in 1768 the British king, George III, decided to send in troops to occupy Boston. The king's hope was that the troops would calm down Boston and also serve as a warning to other colonies not to make trouble.

Two regiments, totaling about 1,000 soldiers, from British posts in Canada sailed into Boston Harbor on six warships in the late fall of 1769. The first ever sent to the colonies in peacetime, the troops marched ashore and took over the Customs House on King Street (now State Street). They set up tents on Boston Common and proceeded to anger the local citizens by stopping and searching innocent people. What made the citizens even angrier was that the city of Boston and the colony of Massachusetts were ordered to pay for the board and lodging of the very troops that had been sent to occupy their city.

As word spread outside Boston that 1,000 British troops were occupying the city of about 15,000 people, men and boys from the surrounding countryside began to make their way to the city. They were not an organized opposition, but they were united in their anger.

Meanwhile, the people of Boston were equally upset. There were minor incidents between the soldiers and the citizens. Snowballs with stones in the centers were thrown at the soldiers, but the soldiers were under orders not to fire their guns. In fact, most of the guns were not even loaded. But they used their bayonets to beat whoever attacked them, and sometimes to beat innocent bystanders.

Two incidents occurred in early 1770 that increased tensions in Boston. In early February a large crowd attacked a Boston man who was known to be friendly to the British. They chased him into his house, and then began to batter down his door with sticks and clubs. The man grabbed his musket and shot into the crowd, killing a twelve-year-old boy named Christopher Snider. The crowd tried to kill the man, but soldiers intervened and took him to jail.

About a month later, on March 2, a British soldier named Killroy walked into a rope maker's shop and asked for a part-time job. The owner wasn't there, but a rope maker named Samuel Gray was. To a man, the rope makers of Boston hated the British soldiers, and Killroy and Gray got into a fight. Other rope makers joined in the beating of Killroy.

When Killroy returned to his barracks, he told his fellow soldiers what had happened. They grabbed sticks and swords and went out after the rope makers, who fought back with iron bars, lengths of rope, and sticks. The wild fight was finally broken up by Boston police and ordinary citizens.

Crispus Attucks was in Boston at that time. A slave named Andrew later said that Attucks had been living in New Providence, in the British colony of the Bahamas, and was in Boston "in order to go [to] North Carolina." The slave Andrew described Attucks as "stout," and since he was over six feet tall he must have been a commanding presence. According to some reports, he was eating supper at a local inn the night of Monday, March 5, when he heard fire alarms and rushed into the street to see what was happening.

Clashes between soldiers and citizens were occurring in several areas that night. A crowd of young men and boys were battling with soldiers on Brattle Street. Around the same time, on King Street, a British private named Hugh Montgomery hit a barber's apprentice in the face after the boy had insulted a British captain. The boy ran through the streets shouting that he had been "killed."

Someone set fire bells ringing, and Crispus Attucks left his supper to investigate.

He made his way to Dock Square, where a large crowd had gathered. Seeing that the people were milling about aimlessly, he picked up a large stick and shouted to the people to follow him to King Street, where the main guard of the British army was stationed. The crowd followed him to the Customs House, where Private Hugh Montgomery had taken up his post as guard.

Some of the boys in the crowd began to taunt Montgomery, whose musket wasn't loaded. The frightened private called for reinforcements, yelling, "Turn out, main guard!" Captain Preston, who was in charge of the guardhouse that day, ordered seven soldiers to go out and help Montgomery. One of them was Private Killroy, who had been beaten by the rope makers. The soldiers used their bayonets as clubs to cut through the crowd and drive it back. Seeing that the crowd was in no mood to retreat, the soldiers loaded their muskets.

The crowd had swelled, as nearly everyone in Boston heard that something was happening on King Street. Samuel Gray, the rope maker, was among those who joined the increasingly unruly mob.

Standing at the front of the crowd was Crispus Attucks. According to the slave named Andrew, who was at the scene, the crowd was crying, "Damn them, they dare not fire, we are not afraid of them." Attucks threw himself into the group of soldiers, said Andrew, and struck at Captain Preston. A group of men followed him, yelling, "Kill the dogs, knock them over."

The soldiers fired. Crispus Attucks was the first to fall, hit by two musket balls. Four other men died: Samuel Gray, the rope maker; James Caldwell, a ship's mate; Samuel Maverick, an apprentice joiner (furniture maker); and Patrick Carr, identified only as an Irishman. Six others in the crowd were wounded, but later recovered.

The next day, the bodies of Attucks and Caldwell were taken to Faneuil Hall, because neither man had a home in Boston. Two days after that, all the shops in the city were closed for the public funeral for the five victims. Thousands of people flocked in from the countryside, and the *Boston Gazette* reported that the funeral was attended by the largest crowd ever assembled in North America.

The coffins of Attucks and Caldwell were carried to meet the hearses with the other coffins on King Street. All the bells in the city tolled in the dead men's honor. There was a long procession to the cemetery, where they were all buried together in one grave.

While some called Attucks and the others heroes, others called them villains. But everyone agreed that Crispus Attucks was the main actor in the event, a stranger who had stepped forward to lead the attack on the soldiers.

The soldiers were placed on trial for the murders of the five citizens. In the bill of indictment that the court brought against the soldiers, the main section was devoted to Attucks, presenting his name first and separately from those of the other victims and charging that he had been assaulted "with force and arms, feloniously, willfully, and of malice aforethought."

John Adams was one of the lawyers for the defense. He would become the second president of the United States, but at the time he was loyal to the king of England. He, too, focused on Attucks, saying that it was to his "mad behavior [that], in all probability, the dreadful carnage of that night is chiefly ascribed." Adams claimed that the soldiers had every right to fear the "stout mulatto fellow, whose very looks was enough to terrify any person."

Captain Preston was found not guilty, since the court ruled that he had acted to protect his troops. Two soldiers were found guilty. As punishment, they were branded in the hand with a hot iron. Those who were against the British did not believe that justice had been done.

Clashes between British soldiers and colonists continued. King George III kept levying taxes upon the colonies without giving them a voice in their own government. Within three years, John Adams had changed his mind and no longer supported the king. He had also changed his mind about Crispus Attucks and the event he called the Boston Massacre.

On a Monday in July 1773, Adams wrote in his diary a letter to Governor Thomas Hutchinson of

Massachusetts. He may have intended to publish it. He wrote it as if it had come from Crispus Attucks:

> *You will hear from Us with Astonishment. You ought to hear from Us with Horror. You are chargeable before God and Man, with our Blood. The Soldiers were but passive Instruments, were Machines, neither moral nor voluntary Agents in our Destruction more than the leaden Pelletts, with which we were wounded. — You was a free Agent. You acted, coolly, deliberately, with all that premeditated Malice, not against Us in Particular but against the People in general, which in the sight of the law is an ingredient in the Composition of Murder. You will hear from Us hereafter.*

Adams signed the letter "Crispus Attucks."

Five years after Attucks's death, the battle of Lexington, with its "shot heard 'round the world," began the War of Independence. But even earlier Attucks's willingness to take a stand for liberty spurred the slaves of Massachusetts to petition for their freedom. Five separate petitions were presented to the governor, the House of Representatives, and the general court in 1773 and 1774. Unfortunately, none of these petitions were acted upon.

When colonial patriots gathered at Lexington

and Concord, Massachusetts, to confront the red-coats from Boston in April 1775, black minute-men were among them. A slave from Lexington named Prince Easterbrooks was one of the first to be wounded at Lexington. Perhaps even more than the white patriots, these black patriots knew what the word *liberty* meant.

Crispus Attucks knew what liberty meant. In 1750 he had seized his own freedom by running away. Twenty years later, he had died fighting for a larger freedom — for himself and for others.

Blacks have honored Crispus Attucks ever since. After the Revolutionary War, black military companies took the name of Attucks Guards. From 1858 to 1870 blacks in Boston held annual Crispus Attucks Days. In 1888 they managed to get the city and state authorities to erect a Crispus Attucks monument on Boston Common. It was the earliest American public monument to a black man.

2
Madam C. J. Walker

Madam C. J. Walker was the first American woman to earn a million dollars. There were American women millionaires before her time, but they had inherited their wealth, either from their husbands or from their families. Madam Walker was the first woman to earn her fortune by setting up her own business and proving that women could be financially independent of men. The company she started in the early years of this century is still in operation today.

Madam C. J. Walker was born Sarah Breedlove on December 23, 1867. She grew up in the South under very racist conditions. Her parents, Owen and Minerva Breedlove, had been slaves until President Abraham Lincoln's Emancipation Proclamation and the Union victory in the Civil War had freed the slaves.

After the war, few provisions were made to help

former slaves become independent. They did not receive money to help them get started in their new lives. They were uneducated, they had few skills except the ability to grow crops, and many were unaware of what freedom meant. Like the majority of former slaves, the Breedloves remained on the Burney family plantation in Delta, Louisiana. They had little choice but to stay on the same land where they had been slaves, only now they were sharecroppers.

Sharecroppers farm land for a landowner. In return, they receive a place to live and part of the crop. But since they must buy what they cannot grow from the landowner, when they harvest the crop they find themselves owing whatever is their share to the landowner anyway.

The Breedloves sharecropped cotton. Like her brothers and sisters, Sarah was working in the cotton fields by the time she was six. By the time she was seven, both her parents were dead, and she moved in with her older sister, Louvenia. A few years later, they moved across the river to Vicksburg, Mississippi.

Sarah had little schooling. Like other sharecroppers' children, she had a chance to go to school only when there were no crops to be planted or harvested, which totaled about four months out of the year. She also had little happiness in her childhood. Not only was she an orphan, but she also suffered at the hands of her sister's cruel husband. Sarah was just fourteen when she married a man named McWilliams to

get away from her sister's household.

By the time Sarah got married, conditions in the South for blacks were actually worse than they had been during slavery. This was the time when Jim Crow laws were passed, segregating southern blacks from whites in nearly every area of life. It was the time when white supremacy groups like the Ku Klux Klan achieved their greatest power, and lynchings of blacks were common.

Sarah and her husband lived with the terror of being black as best they could. In 1885 their daughter, Lelia, was born, and her parents dreamed of making a better life for their little girl. Then, when Lelia was two, McWilliams was killed by a lynch mob.

Sarah was a widow at the age of twenty, and the sole support of a two-year-old daughter. She took in laundry to earn a living and was determined to leave the South. With Lelia, she made her way up the Mississippi River and settled in St. Louis, where she worked fourteen hours a day doing other people's laundry. She enrolled Lelia in the St. Louis public schools and was pleased that her daughter would get the education that had been denied to her. But she wanted more for her daughter and for herself.

Not long after they moved to St. Louis, Sarah McWilliams realized that her hair was falling out. She did not know why, but it is likely that the practice of braiding her hair too tightly was part of the cause. At the time, few hair-care products were available for black women. The ideal was straight, "white," hair, and to achieve this effect black women divided their hair into sections, wrapped string tightly around each section, and then twisted them. When the hair was later combed out, it was straighter. But this procedure pulled on the scalp and caused the hair to fall out.

Sarah was not the only black woman to suffer from hair loss. But she was one who refused to accept the idea that there was nothing she could do about it. For years she tried every hair-care product available. But nothing worked.

Then one night she had a dream. As she told the story many years later, in her dream "a black man appeared to me and told me what to mix up for my hair. Some of the remedy was grown in Africa, but I sent for it, mixed it, put it on my scalp, and in a few weeks my hair was coming in faster than it had ever fallen out." Sarah never publicly revealed the formula of her mixture.

Sarah's friends remarked on what a full and healthy head of hair she had, and she gave some of her mixture to them. It worked on them, too, so she decided to sell it. She later said that she started her "Hair Grower" business with an investment of $1.50.

She had not been in business long when she received word that a brother who lived in Denver, Colorado, had died, leaving a wife and daughters. Her own daughter, Lelia, was attending Knoxville College, a private black college in Tennessee, and did not need her around all the time. Sarah decided to go to Denver to live with her sister-in-law and nieces.

In Denver, Sarah began to sell her special hair-care product and did well. But she realized she needed to advertise to get more customers. Six months after arriving in Denver, she married C. J. Walker, a newspaperman who knew a lot about selling by mail order. With his help, she began to advertise her product, first in black newspapers across the state and later in black newpapers nationwide, and to make more money.

But soon her marriage was in trouble. As Sarah Walker later said of her husband, "I had business disagreements with him, for when we began to make ten dollars a day, he thought that amount was enough and that I should be satisfied. But I was convinced that my hair preparations would fill a long-felt want, and when we found it impossible to agree, due to his narrowness of vision, I embarked in business for myself."

In addition to helping her learn about advertising, her marriage gave Sarah Breedlove McWilliams Walker the name she would use for the rest of her life — Madam C. J. Walker. The "Madam" part was an affectation, but Sarah liked the way it sounded. She thought it would be good for her business. By 1906 her business was so good that she was able to stop doing laundry for a living and devote all her time to her hair-care company. Her products by this time included "Wonderful Hair Grower," "Glossine" hair oil, "Temple Grower," and "Tetter Salve" for the scalp.

Madam Walker was very proud of being a woman, and she was convinced that she could make it in the business world without the help of men. Almost from the start she determined that her business would be run by women. In 1906 she put her twenty-one-year-old daughter, Lelia, in charge of her growing mail-order business. She herself started traveling throughout the South and East selling her preparations and teaching her methods of hair care. She was so successful that two years later she and Lelia moved to Pittsburgh, Pennsylvania, and started Lelia College, which taught the Walker System of hair care.

Once again, Lelia ran the business while her mother traveled thousands of miles to spread the word. Madam Walker realized that the normal outlets for her products — white department stores and pharmacies — were not open to her. These stores would not stock black products because they did not want black customers. In addition to advertising, mostly in black newspapers, Madam Walker had to depend on the institutions in the black communities, the black churches, and the black women's clubs.

Madam Walker's lectures on hair culture were widely attended. She was an excellent speaker and a commanding woman, nearly six feet tall, who was always beautifully dressed and coiffed. She made a lasting impression wherever she went.

Her travels, and her personality, brought her into contact with many important black people. She joined the National Association of Colored Women and through that organization met the educator Mary McLeod Bethune. She also met Ida B. Wells-Barnett, who worked for the right of women to vote, and against lynching in the South. She formed friendships with these women, who helped her spread the word about her business.

Although she lacked the formal education that most of these women had, Madam Walker never felt ashamed of her shortcomings in that area. She taught herself as much as she could and was not afraid to ask someone to define a word she did not know or explain something she did not understand.

There were other black hair-care companies in business at this time. A couple of companies were owned by whites. But they stressed hair straightening. Madam Walker emphasized hair care. Most of the products she developed were aimed at producing healthy hair, not straight hair. She did design a steel comb with teeth spaced far enough apart to go through thick hair, but its main purpose was not hair straightening.

Madam Walker also wanted black women to go into business. Why should they toil over hot laundry tubs and clean white people's houses when they could be in business for themselves? Helping other black women also helped the Walker Company, and with this goal in mind Madam Walker recruited and trained scores of women to use and sell Walker products. Many of them set up salons in their own homes. Others traveled door-to-door selling Walker products and demonstrating the Walker System. Madam Walker insisted that her agents sign contracts promising to abide by her strict standards of personal hygiene — long before various states passed similar laws for workers in the cosmetics field. By 1910 the Walker Company had trained around 5,000 black female agents, not just in the United States but in England, France, Italy, and the West Indies. The company itself was taking in $1,000 a day, seven days a week.

That same year, Madam Walker's travels took her to Indianapolis, Indiana, a city that impressed her so much that she decided to move her headquarters there. She put a man in charge of her operations, which was a departure from her usual philosophy, but Freeman B. Ransom was, in her opinion, an unusual man.

She had met him in her travels when he was working as a train porter summers and during school vacations, while working his way through Columbia University Law School. He impressed her with his ambition and with his vision of progress for blacks. When he finished school, she put him in charge of her Indianapolis headquarters.

In 1913 Lelia moved from Pittsburgh to New York to expand the Walker Company's East Coast operations. Madam Walker built a lavish town house in Harlem at 108–110 West 136th Street and installed a completely equipped beauty parlor.

Lelia had become an astute businesswoman herself, although she did not have the drive of her mother. Lelia, who changed her name to A'Lelia, liked to enjoy the fruits of their success. The Walker town house soon became the "in" place for parties in Harlem, attended by wealthy and artistic people, black and white.

Madam Walker also enjoyed spending the money she made. In 1917 she built a $250,000 mansion on the Hudson River in upstate New York. She hired the black architect Vertner Tandy to design it and named it Villa Lewaro. She drove around in an electric car, dressed in the finest clothing, and was said to have spent $7,000 on jewelry in a single afternoon.

Madam Walker also gave generously to charity. She had a strong interest in education and took time out of her busy schedule to be tutored by Booker T. Washington, founder of Tuskegee Institute in Alabama. She became an avid reader of literature and American history. She encouraged her friend Mary McLeod Bethune and later gave money to Mrs. Bethune to establish her Daytona Normal and Industrial Institute for Negro Girls in Daytona, Florida. When the National Association of Colored Women decided to pay off the mortgage on the home of the late black abolitionist Frederick Douglass, Madam Walker made the largest single contribution.

Madam Walker did not have much of a private life. She spent her time thinking of new ways to increase her business. The friends she had were people who could help her.

By 1917 the years of traveling and overwork began to take their toll on her. She developed high blood pressure, and in 1918 her doctors warned her that she had to slow down. She turned over her responsibilities in the business to her daughter, to Freeman B. Ransom, and to other trusted associates, and retired to her mansion, Villa Lewaro. There, she tried to relax, but her mind was always on her business. She died quietly of kidney failure resulting from hypertension in May 1919.

In her will, Madam Walker left the bulk of her estate and the business to her daughter, A'Lelia. But she also provided generously for a variety of educational institutions run by black women, including $5,000 to Dr. Bethune's school. She established a trust fund for an industrial and mission school in West Africa and provided bequests to Negro orphanages, old people's homes, and Negro YWCA branches. In addition, she made bequests to many friends and employees.

Also in her will, Madam Walker insisted that the Madam C. J. Walker Company always be headed by a woman, and her wishes were carried out. Her daughter, A'Lelia, became president of the company after her death and presided at the dedication of the new company headquarters in Indianapolis in 1927, fulfilling a long-held dream of her mother's.

Times have changed greatly since Madam C. J. Walker made her millions. Drugstores and department stores owned by both whites and blacks now stock hair- and skin-care products for black women. Many more companies, white and black, manufacture such products. In the midst of all that competition, the Walker Company is not as active as it once was, although it still sells some of the products Madam developed. The Walker Building is being renovated as part of the rejuvenation of downtown Indianapolis. Now called the Madam Walker Urban Life Center, it houses professional offices and a cultural center.

Madam C. J. Walker, the daughter of former slaves, with little education, overcame the barriers of being black and a woman and succeeded beyond everyone's expectations but her own.

3
Matthew Henson

Nearly 140 years after Crispus Attucks was the first American to fall in the cause of independence, a black man named Matthew Henson was one of the first two men to reach the North Pole. He accompanied Robert Peary, a white man, on this historic expedition. As recently as 1989, there was some question about whether or not Henson and Peary had reached their goal in 1909. In December 1989 the National Geographic Society announced the results of a study that used new scientific methods to examine Peary's evidence. The study concluded that the evidence proved they had been successful.

Matthew Henson was born in Charles County, Maryland, about forty miles south of Washington, D.C., on August 8, 1866, after the Civil War and slavery had ended. Both his parents were free-born. When he was young, they moved from Maryland to Washington, D.C. The nation's capital had seen a great influx of blacks in the years between 1860 and 1870 as freed slaves and refugees from the South streamed into the city.

Although the District of Columbia was not a state, as the capital of the nation it was looked upon as a model for other southern areas. In 1866, the year of Matthew's birth, all adult men in the District were given the right to vote, regardless of race. Some blacks were elected and appointed to local offices, and in 1869 and 1870 laws were passed that banned segregation in public accommodations such as streetcars and parks.

Matthew's parents believed there was more opportunity in Washington, D.C., but his mother did not live to take advantage of it. She died when Matthew was seven. Matthew then went to stay with an uncle who lived in the District. His uncle sent him to N Street School, one of the first that had opened for blacks. He attended that school until the sixth grade, which was a long time for a child — black or white — to go to school in those days. Most older children had to leave school to go to work to help out their families.

At age fourteen, Matthew Henson got a job to support himself. In those days, many young men went to sea, for there were plenty of jobs in the active shipping business. Matthew went to Balitmore, Maryland, the closest large port, where he shipped out as a cabin boy for Captain Childs on the *Katie Hines*, a vessel bound for China.

As a cabin boy, Matthew cleaned Captain Childs's cabin, served his meals, washed the dishes, and helped the cook. He also helped out in a variety of jobs on board the ship. From the ship's carpenter, he learned to build sea chests and sleeping bunks for the crew. From the ship's mechanic, he learned how the engines worked and how to repair them. From Captain Childs himself, he learned basic navigation skills and much more. In fact, he learned so much about sailing during the months-long voyage to China that in his autobiography he says that after that first voyage he became an able-bodied seaman.

He remained with Captain Childs and the *Katie Hines* and for the next five years traveled to many different parts of the world. From China, he sailed to Japan and the Philippines. He sailed across the Atlantic to France, Spain, North Africa, and southern Russia. Most young men born in America never ventured far from their places of birth, and in the course of his travels Matt acquired an education that he never could have gotten in school.

But Captain Childs saw to it that Matt also received an extensive education from books. He took a personal interest in Matt and determined to give him the education that he was missing by not going to school. The captain had a library filled with books — not just on navigation and geography but on history and literature. He taught Matt as much as he could, and Matt was a willing student. When Captain Childs died dur-

ing a voyage, it was a great blow to young Matt. As he watched the sailors bury the captain at sea, he must have wondered what he would do.

When the *Katie Hines* returned to port in Baltimore, Henson left the ship and decided to try finding a job on land for a while. He hoped to get a job where he could use his skills and his learning, but it was hard for a nineteen-year-old black man to get any kind of skilled job. He worked at whatever he could find around Baltimore, and at various times was a messenger boy, a night watchman, a valet or personal servant to a gentleman, and a stevedore or dock worker.

Eventually he returned to Washington, D.C., where he got a job as a stock boy at B. H. Steinmetz & Sons, a men's clothing store. A young black man would not have been hired to work directly with customers, but Matt Henson was highly intelligent and hardworking, and he had more interaction with the customers than most stock boys would. That is how he met Lieutenant Robert E. Peary, who had come into the store.

Peary, ten years older than Henson, was a civil engineer with the United States Navy. Somehow, he and Matt got into a conversation. Both men liked each other immediately. Peary saw in Henson an eager young man who was intelligent and hardworking, just the type of young man he needed as his personal servant on an upcoming trip to Nicaragua. Henson saw in Peary a man who would take an interest in him, as Captain Childs had, and who had much to teach him.

The reason why Peary was going to Nicaragua was that the Navy wanted to build a canal in Nicaragua to connect the Atlantic and Pacific oceans. Peary's job was to find the best place to dig the canal. They sailed for Nicaragua in November 1887, when Henson was twenty-one years old. On the ship with them were forty-five engineers and 100 Jamaican laborers. Henson was supposed to be Peary's personal servant, but he was soon managing the whole jungle camp. It took seven months in the Nicaraguan jungle for Peary and his crew to complete the survey for the canal, which, as things turned out, was never built. The United States decided later to build the canal in Panama instead.

During the long months in the Nicaraguan jungle, Peary had the opportunity to get to know Henson and to see him at work, and he decided to share with Henson his dream: to lead the first expedition across the ice cap of Greenland.

Back in Washington, D.C., Henson returned to work at Steinmetz & Sons while Peary set about raising money for the Greenland expedition. He still had not raised the necessary money when another explorer beat him to his goal. In September 1889 it was announced that a Norwegian named Fridtjof Nansen had succeeded in crossing the polar ice cap.

About a year and a half later, however, Peary wrote to Henson to tell him of a new plan. Nansen had crossed the southern end of Greenland, but he had not explored the wider, northern part.

Peary decided to do that. He also wanted to see if northern Greenland might lead to the North Pole. Peary reported that he was raising money for the expedition and suggested that Henson join him in Philadelphia, where he was working at the League Navy Yard. Henson immediately gave his notice at Steinmetz's and joined his friend.

At the League Navy Yard, Henson worked as Peary's messenger and watched his progress in raising money for the expedition. Summer was coming, and summer was the only time that a ship could get through the ice to reach Greenland. If Peary didn't leave soon, he would have to wait another year. He confided to Henson that, while he wanted Henson to accompany him, he could not afford to pay him. Would Henson be willing to help him without pay? Henson immediately said yes. He had been practically around the world by sea. He was eager to see what the top of the world looked like.

By this time, Peary had gotten married, and he planned to include his wife in his North Greenland Expedition. In June 1891 the Pearys, Henson, and several other men who had put up money to finance the expedition set sail on the small ship *Kite*, which was outfitted with gear and supplies for eighteen months.

It took the little ship until the end of July to plow through the ice as far north as it could go. It finally dropped anchor in McCormick Bay. Once the supplies were unloaded, the ship sailed for home, leaving the small party of Americans to spend the winter in the barren arctic, waiting for spring and all-day light before making their trip over the polar ice cap.

Henson began to build a small wooden house where they would spend the winter. The others went out to find Eskimos to hire — the men to hunt and the women to make arctic clothing of animal furs and hides. August 8 was Henson's twenty-fifth birthday, and it was the occasion of the first birthday party he'd ever had in his life. Mrs. Peary cooked a feast in his honor, and Henson was deeply touched.

A few days later, when the men returned with a family of Eskimos, he was touched again. The Eskimos saw his brown skin and thought he was one of them. Even though they found out that he didn't speak their language, they called him "Inuit," which was what they called themselves. They referred to him as "Miy Paluk," which meant "dear little Matthew," and taught him the skills of survival in their harsh homeland.

In his autobiography Matthew Henson wrote, "For periods covering more than twelve months, I have been to all intents an Esquimo, with Esquimos for companions, speaking their language, dressing in the same kinds of clothes, living in the same kinds of dens, eating the same food, enjoying their pleasures, and frequently sharing their griefs. I have come to love these people."

He hunted with them and learned how to build snow igloos and how to drive sleds pulled by dogs.

He also took over cooking chores for the party from Mrs. Peary. When spring came, he set out with the other men in the party, plus several Inuit, on the expedition to cross the polar ice cap. But in the course of hauling boxes of food to the ice cap he suffered a frozen heel, and Peary sent him back to the camp to recover and to look after Mrs. Peary.

Only Peary and one other man in the party ended up crossing the polar ice cap. The others could not take the harsh cold, and the Inuit, who feared Kokoyah, the evil spirit of the ice cap, refused to go at all. Peary also discovered a large bay, which he named Independence Bay. He failed, however, to find out if there was a way to reach the North Pole by land.

When the party arrived in New York in September 1892, Peary was greeted with great fanfare. Congratulations poured in, including one from the Norwegian Nansen, who was himself planning an expedition to discover the North Pole. Peary realized he would again be outdone by the Norwegian if he did not raise the money for his own expedition to the Pole soon.

He decided to raise some of the money by going on a speaking tour. Henson accompanied him, along with a sled and six dogs, an Inuit tent, and furs. All were used to illustrate the harshness of life in the north. Peary did the speaking, and Henson illustrated sled driving. The three-month tour raised the needed money, and the second expedition set off from Philadelphia on June 26, 1893, the same day that Nansen's expedition set off from Norway.

This time the party was larger — a total of twelve men, plus Mrs. Peary and a nurse, for Mrs. Peary was expecting a baby. They sailed on the ship *Falcon*, which was stocked not just with food and equipment but also with two St. Bernard dogs, eight burros, and several crates of homing pigeons. The burros were supposed to work as pack animals, but they did not last long in the arctic. Nor did the pigeons, which Peary had hoped to use to send messages.

Henson expected to be included in the expedition to the Pole that set out from camp the following spring. But Peary asked him to remain behind again. This time it was not because of a frozen heel but because Peary believed that only a college-educated man could know what to do in the emergency situations that would arise. Matt Henson never said how he felt about being left behind twice, but there is no question that he was disappointed.

Peary and the others set out for the Pole on March 6, and were back by April 20, having gone only 128 miles. Many of the dogs had frozen to death or gone mad, and the men had become weak. In July 1894 nearly everyone returned to the United States. Mrs. Peary returned because of the new baby. The other men went back because they could not stand the harsh arctic life. Only Hugh Lee and Matt Henson remained with Peary for another try at the Pole.

Peary, Lee, and Henson set off on April 1, 1895, accompanied by three Inuit, six sleds loaded with supplies, and sixty dogs. When they reached the ice cap, they searched for the supplies that Peary had buried the year before, but they were buried so deeply that they could not be found. The Inuit turned back, but Peary, Lee, and Henson pressed on.

They had gone only about fifteen miles when Lee got sick. Peary and Henson had to stop and put up a tent for him. They could barely control the dogs, who were so hungry they attacked the two men. They tried their best to search for a land route to the North Pole, but they did not succeed. By the time they returned to camp on June 25, they had only one dog left and were close to starvation themselves. But Matthew Henson was overjoyed, for he was now the first black man to have crossed Greenland. He had also proved to Peary that, in spite of his lack of a college education, he was a man who could be counted on to meet whatever emergencies came up.

In New York, Henson presented walrus hides he had prepared to the American Museum of Natural History. The curator who accepted the hides was so impressed with the way Henson had prepared the skins that he offered Henson a job. Henson happily accepted and for the next two years he used his great knowledge of arctic life to prepare exhibits for the museum. During the summers of 1896 and 1897 he took time off to accompany Peary back to Greenland to bring back the largest meteorite they had found.

By this time, Peary had decided that there was no land route to the Pole. Instead, he planned to reach his goal by traveling across the frozen Arctic Ocean. He wanted Henson to go with him. Henson enjoyed his job at the American Museum of Natural History and did not look forward to another long period in the harsh arctic North. But he felt that he would bring great honor to black people if he could be with Peary when he reached the North Pole. So he decided to go.

On July 4, 1898, Peary and Henson and one other man, a doctor named Dedrick, set sail on the ship *Windward* on a four-year expedition. Very soon they were in trouble. The ship became icebound 300 miles south of the Arctic Ocean, and they had to unload their supplies and make camp. During the winter, they moved 250 miles overland to Fort Conger. In the course of the move, Peary's feet froze, and he lost all his toes except the two little ones. They pressed on, and spent the next three years searching for a route to the Pole. When the *Windward* returned for them in August 1902, they could claim a record for reaching farther north than any other American. But they had not gotten farther than 343 miles from the North Pole.

Back in New York, Peary began to raise funds for still another expedition. Henson found a job as a pullman car porter on the Pennsylvania Railroad. He planned to marry Lucy Ross, with whom he had fallen in love, but first he wanted to make one more trip with Peary to try to reach the North Pole.

On this trip, which lasted from July 1905 to December 1906, they traveled on a ship, the *Roosevelt*, that was especially designed to smash through ice. Henson and Peary were accompanied by three assistants — a doctor, a teacher, and the captain of the ship. Henson was the arctic expert who, with the Inuit who would accompany them, would teach the others how to survive. On this trip, it was the *Roosevelt* that nearly did not make it. The ship was buffeted by hurricanes and trapped in ice that nearly crushed it, but it limped along until it reached a large body of water in the Arctic Ocean that was not frozen. By the time ice formed, they did not have enough food to continue. They returned to New York having reached a point only 175 miles below the North Pole.

They had come so close that there was no question that they would make another trip. Both Peary, who was fifty, and Henson, who was forty, realized it would probably be their last. Matt wrote in his autobiography, *this time to be the last, and this time to win*. Then he married Lucy Ross.

The repaired *Roosevelt* set sail from New York on July 6, 1908. The party included a teacher, a doctor, a young graduate of Yale University, and two men from the previous expedition, a teacher and Captain Bartlett, the captain of the *Roosevelt*. All of them kept diaries, for they were sure this would be the trip that would make them all famous.

The *Roosevelt* arrived at Cape Sheridan on September 5, and the men made camp and waited until late February to begin the long trip over land and frozen water to the Pole. They took turns blazing a northward trail and then returning to camp to recuperate. By April 1 it was time to cross the last 135 miles of bleak wilderness, and there was no question who would go with Peary — Matt Henson. "I can't get along without him," said Peary. They took four Inuit and forty dogs.

Two days later, Henson and his sled were the first onto a patch of thin ice that broke under the weight, plunging Henson deep into the Arctic Ocean. But one of the Inuit grabbed the hood of his fur jacket and pulled him to safety. After changing his boots and pounding the icy water out of his furs, he pressed on. Three days later, Peary took measurements of their latitude and concluded that they were only three miles from the Pole. They continued on, taking careful measurements at six in the evening, six in the morning, and at noon. At last, Peary was certain that they had reached their goal. He said to Henson, "We will plant the Stars and Stripes — *at the North Pole!*" Henson unwrapped the American flag they had carried with them all those miles, and Peary took a picture of him holding it. Then Peary cut a strip from the flag and buried it in a bottle along with a record of the trip.

They went back to their base camp, having been gone for sixty-eight days.

Henson and Peary spent the next three weeks resting and eating. Henson expected the commander to talk with him about their discovery, and was puzzled when Peary did not speak to him at all. As he wrote in his autobiography,

> *I would catch a fleeting glimpse of Commander Peary, but not once in all of that time did he speak a word to me. Then he spoke to me in the most ordinary, matter-of-fact way, and ordered me to get to work. Not a word about the North Pole or anything connected with it; simply, "There is enough wood left, and I would like to have you make a couple of sledges and mend the broken ones. I hope you are feeling all right."*

Henson did not try to speculate about why Peary behaved that way. Based on Peary's actions and statements later, it is possible that he was worried: What would the world think about his taking a black man with him to the Pole?

On July 18, 1909, the *Roosevelt* began its trip home. During a stop at Etah the group learned that Dr. Frederick Cook, who had been with Henson and Peary on their first expedition to Greenland, claimed he had reached the North Pole in April 1908.

When they returned to New York, they learned that the world was honoring Cook as the discoverer of the North Pole. Peary refused to make any statements to the press and decided to wait for the various scientific societies to study his documents (Cook had not submitted any proof). Henson, on the other hand, told reporters that he didn't believe Cook's claim. He was quoted in *The New York Times* as saying, "Dr. Cook had two inexperienced Eskimos, and he himself knew nothing about sledging over sea ice. . . . Anyone who has traveled over the land ice will tell you that a man who has had no practice sledging over the sea ice could never reach the Pole. It is too hard a proposition for an inexperienced man."

Unlike Peary, Henson was willing to give speeches about the expedition. Wherever he spoke, he impressed his listeners with his knowledge of the arctic. Some, if not many, in the audience went to hear him out of curiosity, to find out why Peary had taken a "colored" man with him. They left understanding why.

Meanwhile, the National Geographic Society finished studying Peary's documents and concluded that he had indeed reached the North Pole. The society awarded Peary and Captain Bartlett gold medals. No mention was made of Matthew Henson.

Peary went before the Naval Affairs Committee, which was considering his promotion to rear admiral. The committee asked him why he had taken Henson to the Pole rather than Captain Bartlett. Peary answered that he had been afraid that Henson would not have been able to return to camp safely without him. He could not bring himself to say publicly that he could not have reached the Pole without Henson.

While Peary enjoyed world acclaim, Matthew Henson had to be content with the honors that came to him from black American groups such as the Colored Commercial Association of Chicago, which gave him a gold medal in 1909, and the group of prominent blacks in New York who gave him a dinner and a gold watch that same year.

Peary retired on a naval pension. Henson went to work as a parking garage attendant in Brooklyn. He later got a job as a clerk at the Customs House in New York and worked there until he retired at the age of seventy.

Henson seems not to have blamed Peary for lacking the courage to tell the truth about his role in the expedition. In 1912, when he published his autobiography, he asked Peary to write the introduction. And when Peary lay dying eight years later, and asked for Henson to come visit him, Henson did so.

The men who had been on the expedition with Peary and Henson knew how important Henson's role had been. Both Captain Bartlett and Donald MacMillan, a teacher, often spoke of his importance to the expedition. In 1937 they saw to it that Henson was invited to join the Explorers'

Club in New York. The following year, Bartlett wrote to Congress asking that a bill be passed to honor Henson, saying, "It is very evident that there is one reason only why Henson has not been honored — he is black." But Congress did not pass the bill.

Not until the 1940s, when the mood of the country began to shift toward greater racial sensitivity, did Henson begin to get the formal recognition he had deserved all along. In 1944, when Congress authorized a medal for all the men in the expedition, Henson was included. The following year, he was honored with a silver medal for outstanding service to the United States.

In 1986 S. Allen Counter, a black professor who was director of the Harvard University Foundation for Intercultural and Race Relations, decided to investigate stories that there were "dark-skinned" Eskimos in Greenland. There he met Matthew Henson's son, Anaukaq, and his family. Anaukaq, Henson's only child, told Counter that a "white-skinned" Eskimo named Kali, the son of Robert Peary, lived nearby.

Counter arranged for both Anaukaq and Kali to travel with their families to the United States to meet their American relatives. The American Pearys refused to attend any of the ceremonies held in honor of the American Eskimos, although eventually Robert Peary, Jr., received Kali for a short time at his home. The American-Eskimo Hensons were proudly and warmly welcomed by the American Hensons, descendants of Matthew

Henson's brothers and sisters. A very happy Anaukaq died shortly after he returned home to
Greenland.

When Peary died, he was buried in Arlington
National Cemetery with other national heroes.
When Matthew Henson died in 1955, he was
buried in a cemetery in the Bronx. But his descendants kept his memory alive and pressed the
government to honor him as it had Peary. At last,
in April 1988 he was re-buried in Arlington National Cemetery, beside Admiral Peary, with a
headstone that reads: "Matthew Alexander Henson, Co-Discover of the North Pole."

4
Marian Anderson

Thirty-seven-year-old Marian Anderson stood in front of the great sculptured figure of Abraham Lincoln and looked out over her audience. The crowd of 75,000 people stretched in a great half circle from the Lincoln Memorial around the reflecting pool and on toward the Washington Monument. She was about to sing an Easter Sunday concert for these people in the capital of the United States, Washington, D.C.

There were police in the crowd. Police on motorcycles had escorted her car to the Lincoln Memorial. There was some fear that there might be trouble. Marian Anderson was a great singer. But Marian Anderson was black. It was 1939, and Washington was a segregated city. So were most of the other cities and towns in the United States.

Marian Anderson had tried to give her concert at Washington's Constitution Hall. But the Daughters of the American Revolution (D.A.R.), who owned the hall, refused to let her. The members of the D.A.R. were descendants of the men who had fought against the British in the American Revolution. But they would not grant a black woman the freedom to perform in their hall.

Many people were outraged at this discrimination. They included Mrs. Eleanor Roosevelt, wife of President Franklin D. Roosevelt. They arranged for Marian Anderson to give her concert elsewhere in Washington. They chose the Lincoln Memorial. As the crowd grew silent, Marian began to sing "America."

That concert on Easter Sunday 1939 became one of the most famous concerts ever given in the United States. It showed the dignity of Marian Anderson, who had been very embarrassed when the D.A.R. would not allow her in their hall. It showed that respected leaders like Mrs. Roosevelt were willing to take a stand against racial discrimination. And it put the idea into the minds of many Americans that maybe it was time to stop treating black Americans like second-class citizens.

It would be years more before segregation was ended. But events like Marian Anderson's concert blazed the trail for equal rights in America.

Marian Anderson was born on February 17, 1902, in South Philadelphia, Pennsylvania. Her father, John, sold coal and ice. Her mother, Anna, was a teacher. After Marian was born, Anna Anderson quit work to care for her baby, although

she took in laundry and did housecleaning to earn extra money for the family.

Two more daughters were born to the Andersons, Alyce and Ethel. The family was poor, but Marian and her sisters did not feel poor. There was much love in the family, and enough money for annual trips to the circus, new bonnets at Easter, and presents at Christmas.

The family all went to church together each Sunday. Both John and Anna Anderson loved to sing, and so did Marian. When she was six, Marian joined the junior choir at the Union Baptist Church. The choir director, Mr. Robinson, thought she had a very good voice, and he asked her and her best friend, Viola Johnson, to sing a duet to "Dear to the Heart of the Shepherd." Marian sang the alto part and Viola the soprano. They were so good that Mr. Robinson had them sing their duet in front of the whole congregation one Sunday.

At school, music was Marian's favorite subject. She learned to read music and to sing different parts. In the church choir she was encouraged more and more by Mr. Robinson. He had her sing duets with her aunt, who was a member of the senior choir. In the junior choir, Marian was now part of a quartet. She always sang the alto line. Among the girls in the choir, there were more who could sing the high notes. So Marian, who could also sing the high notes, was happy to sing the low notes.

Marian's aunt thought she had a wonderful

voice. When a friend who was a preacher decided to start a church of his own, Marian's aunt suggested that her niece sing at a fund-raising concert. They decided to advertise the concert on fliers with Marian's picture and the words, *Come and hear the baby contralto, ten years old*. Actually, Marian was only eight. She also wasn't sure what a contralto was. She knew that alto was the low part. She found out that a contralto was a female singer of the low parts. She had a wonderful time singing at the fund-raising concert.

Also when she was eight, Marian talked her father into buying an old piano. There was no money for lessons, but Marian's music teacher at school or the choir director would give her cards marked with the notes of the tunes she wanted to play, and Marian taught herself enough to play music to sing by.

Then, when Marian was nine, her whole world changed. Her father was working at the Reading Terminal Market, a fresh-fruit-and-vegetable market at the local railroad terminal. He was badly hurt in an accident at work. A few days later, he died. Marian missed him terribly.

Marian and her mother and sisters went to live with her father's parents on Fitzwater Street. In addition to her grandparents, Marian's aunt and two cousins lived in that house, and her grandmother took care of two or three other children while their parents went out to work. Marian enjoyed living in the large, bustling household, but she realized her mother did not want to be a bur-

den on the others. Anna Anderson worked cleaning houses and doing laundry, and she paid rent.
She also kept her family's food separate, so they
would not be eating the grandparents' food.

Marian saw how hard her mother worked and
wanted to help. When she graduated from gram-
mar school and went on to high school, she took
a course that would prepare her to be a secretary.
She knew she would not be able to go to college.

Now, she studied music only once a week. But
she did keep up her singing at church, where she
was a member of the junior choir and, at age
thirteen, the youngest member of the senior
choir. Through the church, Marian also had the
opportunity to hear European music and music
in other languages. She especially liked to hear
Roland Hayes, a black tenor who often sang at
the church's annual concert. One year Marian
was also invited to sing at that concert, and Roland Hayes said he felt she should have professional training. But when he arranged to have
her study in Boston with his own former teacher,
Marian's grandmother said she was too young to
go so far away from home.

When she was still in high school Marian began
to make money through her singing. She sang at
other churches, at the YWCA, and at community
organizations. She turned the money over to her
mother. She joined the Philadelphia Choral Society, a group of black singers, and performed
with them. But she still had no formal training,
and she felt she needed it.

Finally, when she was a junior in high school she met a black music teacher named Mary Saunders Patterson, who agreed to teach Marian free of charge. It was hard for Marian to give up some of her singing habits, but she realized that she must not strain her voice, or else she might someday lose it. She learned how to project her voice to the far corner of a room, to enunciate the words to a song clearly, and to strengthen her voice through special exercises.

Around this time, Marian went to Wilmington, Delaware, to sing at a benefit concert. After the concert there was a reception at the home of a Mr. Fisher. There Marian met Mr. Fisher's son, Orpheus, who was nicknamed "King" and who was about her age. They liked each other and began to visit back and forth. Before long, they were dating. But both were intent on having careers — Marian as a singer and Orpheus as an architect. They would keep in touch, and they talked about getting married someday.

After graduation from high school, Marian decided not to try to get a job as a secretary. She decided to try to register at a music school in Philadelphia. But when she went to the school she was greeted with, "We don't take colored." Years later she said, "That music school no longer exists in Philadelphia, and its name does not matter." But the rejection hurt her deeply, and that did matter. "True enough, my skin was different," she said, "but not my feelings."

With the help of her church, Marian began to

take private lessons with Giuseppe Boghetti, a well-known voice teacher. The church held a gala concert for her and raised $600. Mr. Boghetti taught her how to control her breathing and to sing opera. But she was at a great disadvantage singing in foreign languages because she did not know those languages. She had taken French in school, and Mr. Boghetti helped her with Italian, but she knew no German. She could not afford to pay for language lessons.

Meanwhile, Marian began to sing with an accompanist, a pianist named Billy King. She also took on a manager, G. Grant Williams, who was the editor of a black newspaper in Philadelphia. Williams managed to get her and Billy invitations from outside of Philadelphia to give concerts. They made many trips to the South, where they came up against the strict segregation in that part of the country in the 1920s. They had to travel in railroad cars reserved for blacks and could not eat in the dining cars. Once on a trip to Hampton, Virginia, a storm delayed all the trains, and when Marian and Billy's train finally continued south, black and white passengers traveled together. Everyone got along fine, and Marian wondered why things couldn't be that way all the time.

In 1923, when she was twenty-one, Anderson won a major singing contest in Philadelphia. This win brought her increased attention and more concert bookings. With her earnings, she was able to help her mother buy a house. She was so confident of her singing ability that she decided to take the big step of booking herself into the famous Town Hall in New York, where all the best singers performed. She was so sure she could attract a crowd that she paid for the rental of the hall herself. She expected to get the money back from ticket sales.

On the night of April 23, 1924, Marian and Billy went to Town Hall. She had been told that tickets to the concert were selling well. But when she went out onstage, she saw just a few people scattered through the hall. She tried to overcome her disappointment and give the best performance she could, but she couldn't stop thinking about all the money she had lost. To make matters worse, the few reviews of her concert were poor. One critic wrote that her singing of songs by the German composer Brahms was "as if by rote," meaning that she had memorized the words but had put no feeling into them.

After that disastrous concert, Anderson withdrew completely. She stayed at home and did not even go to her lessons with Mr. Boghetti. She felt as if she had let everyone down. She was certain her singing career was over.

But after a while she realized that she needed to keep making money to help support her family. She swallowed her pride and started singing again. Now, she was determined to improve her ability to sing in foreign languages. She knew the best way to do so was to go to Europe, but she couldn't afford that. She did the best she could by finding people to help her with her pronunciation.

The following year she entered a singing contest in New York sponsored by Lewisohn Stadium Concerts. The prize was to be a recital with the New York Philharmonic Orchestra. There were at least 300 contestants in the first round of the contest. A singer would start to sing, and as soon as the judges had heard enough they would sound a loud clicker and the singer's trial was over. Anderson made it through the first round and made the semifinals with fifteen others.

A few weeks later, she returned to New York for the second round of the contest, at which the sixteen semifinalists would be reduced to four finalists. She had gotten an ear infection from swimming at the YWCA in Philadelphia, and she wasn't sure she should even try. But Mr. Boghetti told her she should go on. Anderson sang three songs, but wasn't sure how she sounded. She was astounded to learn that not only had she won, but there would not even be a final round in the contest.

On August 26, 1925, Marian Anderson sang with the New York Philharmonic Orchestra at Lewisohn Stadium. Unlike the Town Hall concert, this time she had a large audience who applauded enthusiastically. The critical reviews were also better, speaking of the strength of her voice.

As a result of that appearance, one of the top concert managers in the country offered to represent her. She got more invitations to sing and more money for her performances. At last she could support her mother fully. Mrs. Anderson had kept on working and was a night cleaning lady at a department store in Philadelphia at the time her daughter sang with the New York Philharmonic Orchestra. Anderson has always said that the greatest moment in her life was the day she told her mother that she did not have to work anymore.

Through her new agent, Arthur Judson, Marian Anderson met a voice teacher in New York who was able to help with both her technique and her German. But she still felt she would never advance much further in her career unless she went to Europe. She saved her money, and in 1929, when she was twenty-seven, she bought a second-class ticket on the *Ile de France* and set off across the Atlantic Ocean to follow her dream.

Europe was not only a welcoming place for classically trained black singers, it was also where many black jazz singers and musicians went if they could possibly manage it. In Europe, there was no discrimination because of race. There were no segregated railroad cars or buses, so travel from place to place was much easier for blacks than in America. Europeans appreciated black musicians and singers much more than white Americans did. In many cities she visited during her travels in Europe, Anderson found a small number of black American expatriates who had chosen to live and work in Europe because of the freedom and opportunities they enjoyed.

During that first trip abroad, Marian Anderson saw only London, where she studied with a voice teacher who helped her sing German songs, or *lieder*. She would have liked to have stayed longer, and to have gone on to Germany for further study, but she could not afford to. She returned to the United States, and in the fall of 1930 started a new season of concerts with Billy King.

At one of those concerts, in Chicago, a man came backstage and introduced himself as being a representative of the Julius Rosenwald Fund. The fund, set up by a wealthy Chicago business-man, who had been a founder of Sears, Roebuck, & Co., the department store and catalog com-pany, helped blacks by giving them fellowships to pay for their education. Marian Anderson told him about her wish to study in Germany, and soon after she learned that she had been awarded a year's fellowship. She asked if she could take the fellowship in two six-month parts, and was allowed to do so.

Arriving in Berlin, Anderson realized the only German words she knew were the words of songs, but she managed to get by with the help of an English/German dictionary. She studied with a teacher named Michael Raucheisen and in Oc-tober 1930 gave her first German concert at the Bachsaal, a famous concert hall in Berlin. The reviews of that concert were so good that she began to receive invitations to give other concerts in Norway, Sweden, Finland, and Denmark. In fact, the Scandinavians could not get enough of her singing.

After the first half of her Rosenwald fellowship in Europe ended, Anderson returned to the United States hoping that her success would make a difference in the concerts Mr. Judson was able to book for her. But she was still booked at the same churches and colleges and halls where she had performed before. As soon as she had honored her commitments in America, she returned to Europe for the second half of her Rosenwald fellowship. This time she remained in Europe after the fellowship ended and performed all over Scandinavia, giving a total of 116 concerts there. Everywhere she went, audiences cheered and called for more. So loved was she in that part of Europe that one newspaper talked about "Marian fever."

Anderson knew she could never find that kind of success in her own country, and instead of returning to the United States to try to pursue her career, she remained in Europe. She returned home every few months to visit her family, but she did most of her performing in London and Paris and Vienna. However, she never considered moving to Europe permanently, or asking her family to join her there. As she explained years later, "I was — and am — an American."

Sol Hurok, a famous American concert manager, heard Anderson in concert in Europe and asked if he could represent her in her native country. She was delighted at the chance to do concerts in major halls at home. Hurok arranged for her to sing on December 30, 1935, at Town Hall in New York. It was the same hall where she had sung her first concert in that city eleven years earlier. Back then, her concert had been poorly attended and the reviews of her singing had not been very good. But this time she was confident that she would be successful.

Anderson asked her European accompanist, Kosti Vehanen, to go with her to the United States. She worried about traveling with him in the South because he was white. But she felt he could accompany her best. On December 17 the two set sail on the *Ile de France,* the same ship on which she had first sailed to Europe. During that voyage Anderson fell down a flight of stairs and fractured her ankle. She had to wear a cast, but she was determined not to wear it at her concert at Town Hall. She wanted to be judged for the quality of her singing and did not want any sympathy because of her injury.

The night of the concert, she was helped out onto the stage while the curtain was still closed. By leaning on the piano, she could keep most of her weight off her injured ankle. She sang the first half of the concert without most people in the audience knowing that she was in great pain. But her mother and sisters were there, and Mr. Boghetti, her old teacher from Philadelphia, and they knew what courage and strength it took for her to sing. Word had gotten out to a few reporters, and so after intermission she told the audience about her injury. The hall resounded with applause. The next day, the reviews were full of praise.

Sol Hurok arranged several other concerts for Anderson, including one at New York's Carnegie Hall. Offers did not come pouring in, for there were still many halls in the United States where a black singer — even a great black singer — was not welcome. Hurok turned down some offers because he felt Anderson should perform only in the best places and for fees that were appropriate to her stature.

One place at which she performed, in 1936, was the White House. President and Mrs. Franklin D. Roosevelt invited her to give a private recital after a small dinner.

In 1937 Hurok booked her first long tour. It included many appearances in the South, and for the most part Anderson was well received. The halls were in the larger cities, and the audiences were respectful. They even accepted her performing with a white accompanist. However, the halls were segregated, with blacks confined to the balcony. Anderson did not publicly object to performing in these halls, but she made it a point to bow first to the black audience when she came onstage.

Anderson encountered discrimination outside the South as well. She was refused a room in a major hotel in Springfield, Illinois, and also in Atlantic City, New Jersey. Many restaurants refused to serve her and Vehanen. Vehanen found it very difficult to understand why a person's worth seemed to depend on the color of his or her skin. By the time he returned to his native Finland in 1940, he still did not understand racial discrimination in America.

The year before he left he witnessed the most famous case of discrimination in Anderson's career. An Easter Concert in Washington, D.C., in 1939 had been requested by Howard University, a black university in the District. Sol Hurok had tried to reserve Constitution Hall, the major concert hall in the nation's capital, but the Daughters of the American Revolution would not let Anderson sing there because she was black.

The D.A.R.'s refusal made headlines. Important public figures protested. Mrs. Eleanor Roosevelt resigned her membership in the organization. Other members of the D.A.R. protested the decision but the national officers did not change their minds.

Anderson was upset over the whole situation. She was more sad than angry and did not want to be making headlines over such an incident. When the United States Department of the Interior offered her the use of the Lincoln Memorial, she was not sure she ought to accept. "As I thought further," she said later, "I could see that my significance as an individual was small in this affair. I had become, whether I liked it or not, a symbol representing my people. I had to appear."

Anderson's triumphant concert, and all the unpleasantness that led up to it, were an important episode in the history of race relations in the United States. In fact, four years later a large mural depicting the concert was unveiled on the wall of the Department of the Interior building in Washington.

Now Anderson began to insist that blacks in her segregated audiences be offered seats equally as good as the seats for whites. She demanded that blacks be able to buy tickets on a first-come, first-served basis, and not have to wait until whites had been given first chance at the tickets. Eventually, she refused to sing in any concert hall that was segregated.

In 1941 Marian Anderson received the Bok Award, which the city of Philadelphia gave every year to the citizen of whom it was most proud. She was the first black to receive the $10,000 award, which she used to set up the Marian Anderson Scholarship Fund to help music students. She made sure her scholarships went to students of all races so that talent, not skin color, would be what was important. Using her own money, she kept that fund going for the next thirty years.

In July 1943 Marian Anderson married Orpheus "King" Fisher, whom she had started dating when they were both still in school. He had built a career as an architect in New York. Both were in their forties. They bought a farm in Connecticut and named it Marianna Farm. They spent as much time as they could there. Orpheus kept his business in New York, and Anderson continued to travel all over the world giving concerts.

In 1954 Anderson met Rudolf Bing, who was general manager of the Metropolitan Opera in New York. He asked her if she would be interested in singing at the Metropolitan, and although Anderson had never sung in an opera, she immediately said yes. After all, she had sung arias from operas. She wanted a chance to sing an entire role with the greatest opera company in the United States. No black singer had ever sung with the Metropolitan, and she wanted to be the first. Opening night of the opera *A Masked Ball*, January 7, 1955, was a historic occasion. Marian sang the part of Ulrica and when it was over the audience thundered her name.

For nine more years Anderson continued to sing in concerts and operas all over the world, including a tour of Asia sponsored by the U.S. State Department. She was also appointed a member of the United States delegation to the United Nations in New York in 1958. She received many other honors, including the Presidential Medal of Freedom in 1963, before she retired in 1964 to Marianna Farm. She performed occasionally until her death in 1993.

Marian Anderson overcame many barriers to realize her dream to be a singer. By her own example she showed other Americans that talent and dignity and courage are more important than skin color, and she made it easier for the younger black singers of classical music who came after her.

5
Ralph Bunche

In 1950, when he was forty-six years old, Dr. Ralph Bunche became the first black American to win the Nobel Peace Prize. Named after Dr. Alfred Nobel, the Nobel Peace Prize is awarded each year by the Norwegian Parliament and is the highest honor possible for one who has worked for international peace. Ralph Bunche won the prize for his work toward bringing about peace between Israel and its neighbors in the Middle East.

This was not the first "first" for Ralph Bunche, but it was the most special. It made Americans feel proud, but also a bit guilty. Ralph Bunche was being honored by the world when there were still places in his own country where he could not go because he was black.

When Ralph Bunche was born on August 7, 1904, black people were not far removed from slavery. Only forty years earlier, the Civil War had ended slavery, but whites had kept blacks from making much progress. They were segre-

gated in housing, education, and jobs. They were
discriminated against in restaurants and on public transportation. Most, especially in the South,
were not allowed to vote.

Conditions were only a little bit better in the
North, where Ralph was born in Detroit, Michigan. His father, Fred, could not get work in the
city's factories because he was black. Instead, he
earned a living as a baker. But Ralph's grandmother, Lucy Johnson, born a slave, believed that
earning an honest living was the important thing.
That, and how a person felt about himself.

The whole family lived together — Lucy Johnson and her five children. When her daughter,
Olive Agnes, married Fred Bunche, there was no
question that he would move in with his wife's
family. Ralph remembers that the house was
"bubbling over with ideas and opinions" and that
as far back as he could remember he was taught
that education was the best way to get ahead in
life. Work was also stressed, and from the time
he was seven Ralph was running errands for a
neighborhood grocery store and selling newspapers.

Their neighborhood was mostly white. The
Johnsons and Bunches were quite light-skinned
and were thus more easily accepted than darker-
skinned blacks might have been. Ralph's early
friends were the children of German-speaking
Austro-Hungarians who hated Italians far more
than they did blacks.

Ralph was about ten when his mother con-

tracted rheumatic fever. Friends advised that the
damp air of Detroit, which was surrounded by
the Detroit River, Lake St. Clair, and Lake Erie,
was not good for Mrs. Bunche. She needed a
warmer climate. The family talked about moving
to a warmer, drier place and decided on Albuquerque, New Mexico.

Ralph was eleven when the family moved to
Albuquerque in 1915. New Mexico as a state was
only three years old, having joined the Union in
1912. There was a frontier atmosphere about the
place and a strong Spanish influence, because the
area had once been part of Mexico. Ralph's family
moved into an adobe house in a neighborhood
that was mostly black, with a number of Mexican
and Indian families. Ralph did not realize at the
time that Albuquerque was a segregated city.

One day he and his mother, who felt much better in the new climate, went to a movie downtown. As they entered the theater, an usher
approached them and insisted they sit in the balcony. Ralph was astonished. He wondered what
his mother was going to do. Mrs. Bunche would
not be told where to sit. She marched straight
down the aisle to the center of the theater. Ralph
was proud to follow her, and proud of her.

When Ralph entered sixth grade in the Fourth
Ward Elementary School, he found that he was
one of only two blacks in his class of sixty-five
students. He wasn't so sure he was going to like
the school until he got to know his teacher, Miss
Emma Sweet. Miss Sweet loved to teach, and her

students responded by wanting to learn. Ralph made excellent grades and earned the respect of his fellow students. He soon decided that he wanted to become a teacher, like Miss Sweet.

That same year, Ralph's little sister, Grace, was born. Now there was another mouth to feed in the Johnson-Bunche household, and the family was having trouble making ends meet. To help out at home, Ralph got a job in a bakery nearby. Every day after school he would eat a quick supper and then work in the hot kitchen of the bakery until eleven P.M. or midnight. It was hard to keep up with his schoolwork when he was so tired during the day, but he never complained. He wished he could do more for his mother.

In spite of the healthier climate, Olive Bunche's health was getting worse. She died when Ralph was thirteen. Adding to this tragedy, his father died, too, of another illness. Ralph and his little sister, Grace, were orphans.

Fortunately, they still had their grandmother, Lucy Johnson, whom everyone called Nana. She decided it was time to move to a new place, to make a new start. She had heard that there was opportunity in California, and she soon moved the whole family to Los Angeles.

In that California city Ralph learned more about racial prejudice. His uncle Ralph had rented a small house in a predominantly white neighborhood, but when the family arrived to move in they found the door locked. The landlord saw them coming and realized they were black.

Nana would not bow to racism. They had paid
one month's rent, and she ordered her nephew to
break down the door. But when the month was
over, they moved to a house in another mostly
white neighborhood. They met with some hostil-
ity there, too, but they stayed.

Ralph enrolled at Thirtieth Street Intermediate
School and soon decided he didn't like it. Instead
of being offered courses that would prepare him
for college, he was placed in classes where prac-
tical, commercial subjects were taught. When
Nana found out, she went to the principal and
insisted that Ralph be switched to an academic
course. He was able to take algebra and geometry,
natural science, history, and French, and he began to like school again.

After school he peddled papers for the *Los Angeles Times*. During summer vacations he worked
as a house servant in Hollywood homes or in the
kitchens of beach hotels. The summer he was
fourteen, the *Times* sponsored an outing for all
the newsboys at a pool in nearby Venice, California. But when the boys made for the pool,
Ralph and Charlie Matthews, the only two blacks,
were stopped at the gate: No Negroes allowed.
Ralph and Charlie sat on a bench and watched
the other boys having fun in the pool. They were
so embarrassed that they tried to shrink down on
the bench so they wouldn't be noticed.

Ralph entered Jefferson High School. While the
school was predominantly white, most of Ralph's
close friends were black. He hung around with a

group of fifteen or twenty other students. One of their favorite activities was integrating local soda parlors. They would enter one of the parlors and sit at the counter until they were served. Sometimes that took all day, but they usually won.

In spite of having to work, Ralph made excellent grades in high school, and in his senior year he expected to be named to the citywide scholarship honor society. So did the rest of his class, since he had the highest grades. But when the list was read, Ralph's name was not on it.

This was a form of racism he could not understand. Most of the discrimination he had suffered before had been impersonal — because he was black. But this case involved prejudice against *him*. Everyone in the school knew him and knew his academic record. He was so angry that he wanted to leave school, but he realized that he would only be hurting his chances to go to college.

At the end of the year Ralph was named valedictorian of his class because he had the highest grades. But he was surprised to learn that he had also been chosen as commencement speaker. He just shook his head, wondering if he would ever understand white people.

Ralph's fine academic record earned him a scholarship to the University of California at Los Angeles (UCLA). At first he wasn't sure if he should go to college. Very few of his classmates were going, and he wondered if he could measure up. Also, he knew his family could use the money he made from working. He considered remaining at his summer jobs — laying carpets by day and doing janitorial work at night. But his grandmother would not hear of his working. "My grandson is going to college," she said.

The scholarship paid for tuition and books, but Ralph had to work for room and board and other expenses. He found a basement room near the university that he could have rent-free in exchange for doing odd jobs around the building. With another student, he started a cleaning service, which gave him money for food and other expenses.

In spite of working two jobs, he still managed to make good grades, which made him eligible to participate in sports at the university. He played football, baseball, and basketball during his freshman year.

From time to time, Ralph encountered racism at UCLA. On one occasion he was barred from the university debating society because he was black. Several members of the society objected, and when they could not make the society admit Ralph, they quit and formed their own debating society. They elected Ralph president.

In his senior year Ralph was elected to Phi Beta Kappa, the national honor society. He graduated from UCLA *magna cum laude*, with high honors. He also received a fellowship for graduate work at Harvard University in Cambridge, Massachusetts.

The fellowship covered only tuition, and Ralph wondered how he was going to pay his other expenses, including his trip from California to Massachusetts. But by this time he was something of a hero in the black community in Los Angeles. A local social club held a benefit for him and presented him with one thousand dollars.

Ralph had never been so far from home, but he was determined to do well at Harvard. He was one of the few black students there and was treated with great consideration. In fact, while before Ralph had succeeded *in spite of* his color, now he was being helped *because of* his color. But going to school at Harvard was no free ride. He worked at a bookstore near the university to earn money for his expenses and spent long hours studying for his courses in government. In 1928, when he was twenty-four, he earned his master's degree in government and a fellowship for further study.

He had started taking courses toward his doctoral degree when his beloved Nana died. He was deeply saddened to lose her, but he was happy she had lived long enough to see him get the education of which she had dreamed.

Before continuing with his work toward his Ph.D., Bunche accepted an offer from Howard University to organize a new political science department. He was excited by the idea. Besides, he felt he needed a break from studying. And, he could use the money.

Howard was an old and respected black institution of higher learning, but it didn't have much money. That is why a young, inexperienced man like Bunche was asked to start a whole new department. Also, there were very few blacks in the country who had managed to earn a master's degree in government. Some older professors at Howard wondered if Bunche was up to the job. They soon learned that he was.

During his first year at Howard, Bunche met Ruth Harris, a native of Montgomery, Alabama, who was teaching elementary school in Washington, D.C., and taking graduate courses at Howard. Bunche had not had much time for romance, but when he found the right woman it did not take him long to marry her. Ruth Harris became Mrs. Ralph Bunche the following June.

Washington, D.C., was a very southern, segregated city in 1929, when Bunche arrived. The conditions in which most of its black citizens lived were terrible. Soon they were even worse. The stock market crashed in the fall of 1929, and the Great Depression that followed was much harder on blacks than on whites. Many lost their jobs. But what bothered Bunche most was the segregation, which existed in good economic times and bad. He did not like the idea that in the capital of the United States blacks were denied service in restaurants, made to sit in separate sections of theaters and streetcars, and not allowed to use public libraries and parks.

He served on committees protesting discrimination by department stores and theaters. He also joined the local branch of the National Association for the Advancement of Colored People

(NAACP), which worked against segregation.

Meanwhile, he took courses at Harvard during the summer and in 1932 went abroad for several months of study on a grant from the Rosenwald Fund. In 1934, at the age of thirty, Ralph Bunche received his Ph.D. in government and international relations from Harvard. He was the first black man in the country to receive a Ph.D. in political science.

He returned to Howard to teach for two more years. But he wanted to do more study abroad. By this time he and Ruth Bunche had two daughters, Joan and Jane, and he knew that he should earn a steady salary and stay home with his family. But he was eager to learn more about the world, and his wife understood his need to know. In 1936, the same year he published his first book, *World View of Race,* Bunche took a leave of absence from Howard and set off for London and South Africa. His expenses were paid for by a two-year grant from the Social Research Council.

His experience in South Africa was both painful and joyous. He was deeply angered by the way blacks were treated by the white South Africans who were in power. Segregation there was far worse than it was in the United States. But he was also delighted at the warmth of his reception from the African villages he visited.

When he returned to the United States in 1938, Bunche began to work with Swedish sociologist Gunnar Myrdal. Myrdal was doing a survey on the Negro in America, and Bunche took the opportunity to learn more about his own people in his own country. The two traveled throughout the South interviewing people, black and white. They found a huge gulf between the races, and so much discrimination against blacks that it was hard to imagine America ever being anything but a divided country.

Bunche returned to Howard University in September 1941, but when he was offered a job with the United States Coordinator of Information, he took it. Shortly after he started that job, Japan bombed the U.S. naval base at Pearl Harbor, Hawaii, and the United States entered World War II. Most of Bunche's work had to do with preparations for the invasion of North Africa. In June 1942 he became chief of the African section.

Two years later Bunche transferred to the State Department, where he was the first black ever to hold a desk job.

The State Department was working on U.S. plans for a new world organization called the United Nations. They needed someone who knew about colonies and other dependent territories. Bunche did much to bring about the birth of the United Nations. There were many problems in setting up this attempt at a world government. Many countries, large and small, were suspicious of sharing power.

Meanwhile, the Bunches had a third child, a son whom they named Ralph, Jr. They tried to live as best they could in Washington, D.C., but segregation remained an ever-present fact of life.

Their daughters had to be bused to a black school three miles from home because they were not allowed to attend the all-white grade school near where they lived.

As a member of the State Department and as one of the organizers of the United Nations, Bunche could have used his position to speak out against segregation. He chose instead to concentrate on questions of peace and justice in the larger world.

World War II ended with the defeat of Nazi Germany in Europe and Japan in the Pacific. But there was still much unrest in the world, and there were many changes in the nations of the world as a result of the war.

In the early months of 1946, the Bunches moved to New York City, where Bunche went to work for the United Nations as director of the trusteeship division.

In June 1947 Bunche visited Palestine with a U.N. Special Committee that later recommended that the area be partitioned. Since 1923 Palestine had been under the control of the British, but they were willing to turn it over to the United Nations. Under the partition agreement, one-third of the area would become the new state of Israel. One-third would be an Arab state. And one-third, including the holy city of Jerusalem, would be an international zone.

The neighboring Arab countries vowed to fight to prevent partition and attacked the Israelis. The United Nations now faced the challenge of solving the Palestine problem. The major powers were not willing to use force to end the fighting that had broken out. The General Assembly of the U.N. appointed a mediator, Count Folke Bernadotte, a member of the Swedish royal family. Bunche, as director of the trusteeship division, headed the U.N. staff serving under Count Bernadotte.

Count Bernadotte managed to negotiate a temporary truce. But on September 17, 1948, near Jerusalem, he was assassinated. The fragile truce soon ended.

The Secretary General of the U.N. appointed Bunche as acting mediator, and he worked hard to bring about another truce. He told reporters that he intended to get a negotiated treaty signed. He vowed, "I'll never adjourn this meeting. I'll stay for ten years if necessary."

Many issues were at stake. There were issues of religion and race, not to mention national pride, to get past before there could be talk of peace. At first, Bunche met with each side separately. Then he started having meetings between the Israeli delegation and one Arab delegation at a time. When he wasn't conducting these meetings, he was preparing for them, working long hours and far into the night. He also had to contend with charges that he favored one side over the other. But all sides realized that he had experienced racism and discrimination himself and had a better understanding of the problems in the Middle East than many white Americans would have had.

It took eighty-one days for Bunche to get the four armistice agreements necessary to end the fighting. But he succeeded, and praise poured in from all over the world.

Asked by reporters to speak of his role in bringing about a truce in Palestine, he referred to the charges that had been made about his being biased in favor of one side or the other. He said, "I do, indeed, have a number of strong biases. I have a deep-seated bias against hate and intolerance. I have a bias against racial and religious bigotry. I have a bias *against* war; a bias *for* peace."

Bunche took the occasion to talk about the racial problem in the United States, saying,

> *I cannot avoid reminding my fellow Americans that all of us who have a sense of justice and fair play must contribute to the solution of a problem on our doorstep which is perhaps more complex and baffling than the Palestine problem, if our own great country is to be enabled fully to live up to the principles of the charter to which all of the United Nations are solemnly pledged.*

For his work in bringing about a truce in Palestine, Ralph Bunche was awarded the Nobel

Peace Prize in 1950. It was the greatest of many honors he received after he returned home.

Bunche continued to work for the U.N. In 1955 he was named Under Secretary of the United Nations. He worked hard to maintain the fragile peace in the Middle East, which kept being threatened by one side or the other. He worked to guide former African colonies to independence.

Meanwhile, in the United States, the nonviolent civil rights movement began and made great progress under the leadership of Dr. Martin Luther King, Jr., and others. Bunche supported the movement and walked beside Dr. King during the Selma-to-Montgomery March in Alabama in 1965, a march to demand voting rights for blacks in that state.

Bunche devoted the rest of his life to his work for international peace. When he retired from the U.N. in June 1971, at the age of sixty-seven, it was because he was in very poor health. He died six months later, on December 9.

In his own country, Ralph Bunche was never as famous as Martin Luther King, Jr., or Malcolm X. He never wanted fame and to the end refused to write his own life story. Noting that Bunche was not the typical American hero, the magazine *Progressive* stated, "When such men as Dr. Bunche . . . also become 'great heroes' in the eyes of millions of Americans, we will be approaching maturity as a nation. . . . Until the world's peacemakers become our heroes, too, we will not have achieved that maturity."

6
Charles R. Drew

Charles Richard Drew gave the world the techniques for isolating and storing blood plasma. These techniques made it possible to hold blood for long periods of time and for use in emergencies. He helped to save thousands of white and black lives in a time when many blacks died because white hospitals would not treat them.

Charles Richard Drew was born on June 3, 1904, in Washington, D.C. He was the first child born to Richard Thomas Drew, who made his living as a carpet layer, and Nora Rosella Burrell Drew, a teacher. The Drews had four other children after Charles Richard, and Mrs. Drew stopped work to stay at home and care for them.

The area of Washington where the Drews lived was called Foggy Bottom, located along the Potomac River. Originally a small fishing village, it was swampy and often unhealthy. The poorest residents of the city lived there. Many former slaves and free blacks had moved there before the Civil War. After the war they were joined by Irish, Italian, and German immigrant families. By 1900 it was one of the worst slums in Washington, filled with wooden shacks and unpaved streets.

The Drews were poor. It was hard for Thomas Drew to take care of his family on his earnings as a carpet layer, especially after the other children were born. But the Drews were proud people. Thomas Drew taught all his children, "Do what you believe in. Take a stand and don't get licked." Nora Drew taught her children to respect the value of an education.

Very close to where the Drews lived were farms where racehorses were trained, and as a boy Charlie often visited the farms. He got to know the trainers and learned how to care for the horses. Sometimes he was allowed to ride them, which he loved to do. While most boys dream of growing big, Charlie hoped that he would remain small so he could become a jockey. In the early days of horse racing, more blacks than whites were jockeys. Unfortunately for Charlie, but luckily for the world, Charlie grew too big to be a jockey. In college, when he had reached his full growth, he was 6'1" and 195 pounds.

He was athletic from a very young age. At Stevens Elementary School he played football and baseball. Stevens was built as a colored public school in 1868 and still stands on Twenty-first

Street between K and L streets in Washington. When Jimmy Carter was president, his daughter Amy enrolled at Stevens in 1976.

After graduating from Stevens Elementary, Charlie went to Dunbar High School, an all-black school with a fine reputation for turning out well-educated students who went on to college. There, he continued to play sports. In fact, he won letters in baseball, basketball, football, and track. Toward the end of his high school career, he won the James E. Walker Memorial Medal as an outstanding all-around athlete.

Because his family needed the help, Charlie got his first job at the age of twelve. He took on a newspaper delivery route, which he managed to build up so much that by the time he graduated from high school he had six other boys working for him. On graduating from Dunbar, his grades and his skill as an athlete won him a scholarship to Amherst College in Amherst, Massachusetts.

The small private men's college was a mostly white school that stressed academics. But at the time Charlie enrolled, the school was beginning to pay more attention to its athletic program. Charlie helped to make it a great school for athletics.

In his junior year Charlie was named an All-American halfback and won the Thomas W. Ashley Memorial Trophy as the Most Valuable Player on Amherst's football team.

When he graduated in 1926, he was presented with the Howard Hill Mossman trophy for his contributions to Amherst sports during his college career.

As a star athlete, Charlie was very popular at Amherst, and his popularity helped shield him from the racism a less athletic black student might have encountered. But even Charlie did not escape racism altogether. One time the track team went to Brown University in Providence, Rhode Island, for a meet. When the meet was over, the team went to the Narragansett Hotel in Providence for dinner. But the hotel would not allow Charlie and the three other black members of the team to eat there. They had to go back to the Brown University dining hall. Charlie knew that no matter how good he was, he was still judged first by his skin color.

While at Amherst Charlie had become interested in science and started thinking about becoming a doctor. He wanted to go to medical school, but there were no scholarships available to him and he did not have enough money for the tuition. So to save up the money, he accepted a job as Director of Athletics at Morgan State University, a black college in Baltimore, Maryland. He also taught biology. During his two years at Morgan he coached both the football and basketball teams to championship level. But after the two years were up, he applied to Howard University Medical School.

Howard was a black university founded in 1867 and located in Washington, D.C. Established during the Reconstruction period to educate blacks who had been denied the opportunity to go to college, it was an old and respected institution, many of whose graduates went on to become great leaders. But Charles Drew was one future leader whom Howard would not be able to claim. The medical school rejected him. The reason, he was told, was that he did not have enough undergraduate credits in English. What Howard did offer him was a job as an assistant football coach, but Drew was determined to go to medical school and become a doctor.

He next applied to the medical school at McGill University in Montreal, Canada, a fine school which had a reputation for accepting black students and treating them well. He had no trouble being accepted there.

At McGill, Drew continued to participate in sports. He won many Canadian championships, and as captain of the track team achieved the all-time top score at McGill in intercollegiate track competition.

Charles Drew would always be glad he went to McGill instead of Howard, for at McGill he became interested in what turned out to be his life's work.

His instructor in anatomy was John Beattie, a young British doctor who was studying the techniques and problems of blood transfusion. Before the 1930s people often died from loss of blood after accidents or surgery. Researchers had been studying the idea of replacing the lost blood with blood from other people. But they had found that the human body would reject blood that was not similar to its own.

Dr. Karl Landsteiner, born in Vienna but working at the Rockefeller Memorial Institute in New York City, had been working on this problem of rejection. He discovered that all people have one of four different blood types, which he called A, B, AB, and O. A person who had suffered a loss of blood would not reject the blood of a donor whose blood matched or was compatible with his. Landsteiner won the Nobel Prize for Medicine in 1930 for his discoveries.

The problem was that there wasn't always time to find a donor with matching or compatible blood. That was the problem that interested Dr. Beattie at McGill University and that, in turn, interested Charles Drew. They wanted to find a way to make blood readily available in emergencies.

Drew almost had to interrupt his schooling at McGill University. He ran out of money. The stock market had crashed in New York City in 1929, and the Great Depression that followed had affected not only the United States but the rest of the world as well. Jobs were very scarce, and Drew couldn't seem to find work. Then he learned about the Julius Rosenwald Fund.

Drew applied for a Rosenwald Fund fellowship to continue in medical school, and he received enough money to finish at McGill. The year he graduated he was second in his class of 137 students. He also won two major prizes. One was the annual prize in neuroanatomy, the study of the structure of the nervous system. He won the other prize, the Williams Prize, by taking a special examination and scoring among the five highest in the class.

After graduation Drew did his internship at the Royal Victoria and Montreal General hospitals. He then did a year's residency at Montreal General. John Beattie, his instructor at McGill, was also at Montreal General at the time, and the two continued to research ways to store blood for emergency transfusions. But in 1935 the two parted ways. Beattie returned to England. Charles Drew accepted a positon at Howard University Medical School as an instructor in pathology.

Drew was very successful teaching at the medical school that had denied him admission as a student. He worked at Freedmen's Hospital, the teaching hospital of the university, and was quickly promoted to assistant in surgery and then to assistant surgeon. After three years at Howard he was awarded a Rockefeller fellowship to continue his own studies, and he enrolled at Columbia University in New York City.

Arriving at Columbia in 1938, thirty-four-year-old Charles Drew began a residency in surgery at Columbia Presbyterian Hospital, the university's teaching hospital. He also devoted his research to further studying blood transfusions and the storing of blood. In the course of his research he discovered that plasma, the liquid portion of blood that does not contain cells, could be dried and stored for long periods of time without deteriorating. He realized that blood plasma could be the basis of emergency blood supplies, and in 1939, with the aid of a grant from the Blood Transfusion Association in New York City, he set up a blood bank at the hospital. This blood bank stored deposits of blood for times when it was needed.

His work in the field was exciting to the medical community, and in April 1939 Drew was asked to present a report on his research at Tuskegee Institute, an all-black college in Alabama. On his way to the conference he stopped in Atlanta, Georgia. There, he met a young teacher at Spelman College named Lenore Robbins and immediately fell in love. On his way back from the conference he proposed to her. They were married in September, settled into a comfortable home in Washington, D.C., near Howard University, and started a family. They would eventually have three girls: Bebe Roberta, Charlene Rosella, and Rhea Sylvia.

The following year, 1940, Drew became the first black man in the United States to be awarded a doctor of science degree. His thesis was on "Banked Blood."

Meanwhile, World War II had broken out in Europe. Nazi Germany had taken over Poland and France and was threatening England. Dr. John Beattie was now Director of Research Laboratories at the Royal College of Surgeons in London and in charge of blood transfusions for the Royal Air Force. He was running short of blood to treat the wounded, so he cabled to his former student for help.

First Drew traveled to England with thousands of pints of dried plasma. Then he was named medical supervisor of blood for Great Britain. He organized a huge project sponsored by the Blood Transfusion Association in New York and involving major American hospitals to supply Great Britain with all the blood plasma it needed.

This meant organizing a system of volunteer blood donors, centralizing the collection of donated blood, processing the blood and separating out the plasma, drying and storing the plasma, and transporting huge quantities of it across the Atlantic to England. Drew had the system running smoothly by 1941, when the project was taken over by the American Red Cross.

By the time the Red Cross took over, the United States had entered World War II. Charles Drew was made director of the blood bank in New York. He was also named assistant director of blood procurement for the National Research Council, in charge of collecting blood for the U.S. Army and Navy.

Now that the lives of U.S. soldiers were at stake, the ugly racism of America reared its head. Some whites did not want their wounded sons and brothers receiving blood from black people. Even though there was no scientific evidence that blood from different races was different blood, these people were powerful enough to push through a policy of segregated blood banks. The Army, Navy, and Red Cross freely admitted that the new blood segregation policy was not based on scientific evidence but on political pressures.

This policy made blood collection and processing much more difficult. White blood and black blood had to be collected, processed, and stored separately. Only white blood could be used in transfusions for white patients; only black blood in transfusions for black patients. Not only was this procedure costly in time and effort, but it went against everything Charles Drew had learned about medicine. As he said in 1942, "I feel that the recent ruling of the United States Army and Navy regarding the refusal of colored blood donors is an indefensible one from any point of view. As you know, there is no scientific basis for the separation of the bloods of different races except on the basis of the individual blood types or groups." Charles Drew was in the business of saving lives, and he resigned from the program.

Drew had been anxious to get back to surgery anyhow, and he returned to Howard University as a full professor and head of surgery at the medical school. He was also made chief of surgery at Freedmen's Hospital. He served with such distinction that each year brought more honors, including election to the International College of Surgeons in 1946.

In 1949 the United States Government appointed him a surgical consultant for the Army's European Theater of Operations. He toured Europe as part of a four-man medical team looking into conditions at hospitals there and suggesting ways to improve them. Returning to the United States, he was in constant demand at conferences and meetings all over the country.

In late March 1950 he was invited to attend a meeting at Tuskegee Institute in Alabama. He gave his speech and was anxious to get on the road for home. But there were various delays, and he did not set off until two o'clock in the morning. Three other doctors were with him in the car. Drew was driving. All were exhausted, and in Burlington, North Carolina, Drew fell asleep at the wheel. The car ran into the shoulder of the road and turned over. Drew was killed instantly. The others suffered only minor injuries.

In his short life Dr. Charles Drew did more for humanity than most medical men could do in two full lifetimes. He was more fortunate than many other black pioneers in that his contributions were recognized during his lifetime, although international respect did not shield him from racism. Today many of the techniques he developed for storing and transfusing blood continue to be used, and in 1981 his portrait appeared on the thirty-five-cent postage stamp.

7
Romare Bearden

Romare Bearden was born into a middle-class family and never suffered real poverty. He was raised in the North and did not have to contend with the segregation of the South in the first half of this century. He became the most celebrated black American artist of the twentieth century. But because he was black he had to struggle for much of his career to get his work shown. And throughout his career he had to struggle against being labeled a black artist.

Following Bearden's death in 1988, a writer named Amei Wallach published a newspaper article in appreciation of his work and career. "Instead of recognizing the sheer technicolor brilliance of his work, critics confined him to an artistic ghetto," wrote Wallach. "America's greatest black artist is what they called him. It meant that his art — unlike that of most black artists — got looked at. But it wasn't always seen for what it was."

White people who saw that his subject matter was often black people appreciated his forms and colors, but didn't think that his vision of life could have anything to do with them. Bearden spent his whole career trying to create a vision of life that went past race. He never succeeded in getting most people to see it.

Romare Bearden was born in Charlotte, North Carolina, on September 2, 1912. Charlotte was where Romare's father's family came from. Romare's parents, Howard and Bessye J. Bearden, actually lived in New York, in Harlem, where Howard worked for the City of New York as a sanitation inspector and Bessye was New York editor of the black weekly newspaper, the *Chicago Defender*. The name they gave their only child, Romare, is pronounced "Romery" and is a West Indian name, for both parents were of West Indian heritage.

Romare grew up in Harlem. At that time, Harlem was just beginning to be a black neighborhood.

Romare and his family lived on the third floor of an apartment building at 154 West 131st Street. With both parents working, and only one child, the family lived comfortably. Romare went to Public School 139 at 140th Street and Lenox Avenue, in the heart of Harlem. His classmates were a mixture of blacks and white immigrants, mostly Italian and Irish. Whole blocks of Harlem were Italian or Irish or African American, and there was not much mingling outside of school.

In fact, black kids stayed away from the white blocks and vice versa. Romare was sometimes at a disadvantage because he was so light-complected as to be taken for white. He ran the risk of being beaten up by the white kids because he was a Negro and of being beaten up by black kids he didn't know because they thought he was white.

Except for having to worry about the gangs and their turf wars, life in Harlem was exciting for a young boy. Bearden remembered that the sound of jazz was all around: "Not only was it on the radio and record players, but I often heard sounds of a piano from an open window, and in warm weather there were likely to be two or three musicians on a street corner playing for whatever onlookers might drop in the hat. . . . J. Rosamond Johnson [a great black composer] lived in the same apartment house as my parents; among the many, many compositions he wrote with his brother James Weldon is 'Lift Every Voice and Sing,' which became the Negro National Anthem."

Romare's father was musical and as a young man had been the organist in his church in Charlotte, North Carolina. In Harlem, he made friends with many great musicians. The composer and orchestra leader Duke Ellington was one of them. From time to time, Romare thought of composing songs, but he was not very serious about it.

When Romare was small he spent his summers in North Carolina with his father's relatives.

When he was around ten he began visiting his mother's people in Pittsburgh, Pennsylvania, each summer. His grandmother lived near the steel mills and ran a boarding house for the black men who came from the South to work in the mills. The men could make $40–$50 a week, far more than they could make at any job in the South. But working around the hot furnaces was hard. Romare remembered his grandmother rubbing down the men's bodies with cocoa butter, because they would be scorched from the flames of the furnaces.

The summer he was twelve Romare met the person who introduced him to art. The boy's name was Eugene, and he wore leg braces, having suffered from infantile paralysis. He could not run and play with the other boys, but he could draw beautifully. Romare asked Eugene to teach him. Romare's grandmother set up a table in his room, and every day he and Eugene would draw. All of Eugene's drawings were of the local house of prostitution, which was called Sadie's, and when Romare's grandmother saw the drawings she took them away. After she learned that Eugene's mother worked at Sadie's, she insisted that Eugene come to live with them. His mother seemed pleased with the idea and visited on Sundays.

Eugene stopped drawing after he went to live with Romare's grandmother. He was sickly and died about a year later. Thirteen-year-old Romare was a pallbearer at his funeral.

Romare attended one year of high school in Harlem, but after that he decided he would rather be with his friends in Pittsburgh. His parents had no objection, and he lived with his grandmother while attending Peabody High School. He graduated in 1929, the year the New York stock market crashed.

The Great Depression soon followed, but it did not really affect Romare's family. His father did not lose his job. His mother had by this time become a community leader, the first woman appointed to a school board in New York City and chairwoman of the local school board. She was also national treasurer of the Council of Negro Women and a member of the executive board of the New York Urban League. They had the money to send Romare to college, and there was no question that he would go. His parents wanted him to be a doctor.

Romare first enrolled at Boston University. There, he devoted more attention to baseball than he did to his studies. He was the star pitcher on the varsity team. During the summers, he pitched for the Boston Tigers, a Negro team that often played exhibition games with semipro clubs. In those days, there were no blacks in major league baseball, but because he was so light-skinned Romare was told that if he wanted to he could pass for white and join a major league team. But he did not want to do that.

At the urging of his parents, after two years in Boston Romare transferred to New York University. There, he settled down to his studies and majored in mathematics with the idea of going on to medical school. He also started drawing for the college humor magazine.

From time to time in the years after Eugene's death, Bearden had sat down to draw, but he hadn't devoted much time to it while he was playing baseball. Now, he started getting interested in it again. He met E. Simms Campbell, a very successful black cartoonist, who saw talent in his work and encouraged him to pursue it. Soon, Bearden was contributing a weekly political cartoon to the *Afro-American*, a nationally circulated black newspaper based in Baltimore, Maryland.

By the time Bearden graduated from NYU in 1935 with his degree in mathematics, he had given up the idea of being a doctor. His mother, especially, did not want him to be an artist. She told him that there were very few black artists and that he would be hard-pressed to make a living from his art. The same year Bearden graduated from NYU, his mother got a job as Deputy Collector for the Third New York Internal Revenue District. She firmly believed that a person should either have a government job, as she and her husband did, or become a professional, such as a doctor. But Bearden was determined to do what he wanted.

That same year he attended a meeting of artists at the Harlem YMCA on 135th Street and was delighted to see some forty to fifty people there. There were obviously more black artists around than his mother thought. Some of them formed the Harlem Artists Guild, and Bearden found the guild to be an important source of moral support, not to mention artistic influence.

By this time the Great Depression had plunged the nation into hardship, and the federal government under President Franklin D. Roosevelt was trying to provide jobs in a variety of fields. These included art, writing, and theater. The Works Progress Administration (WPA) set up programs to pay writers and other artists to create works for the people, and many of Bearden's artist friends worked for the WPA. Unfortunately for Bearden, his parents made too much money for him to be eligible.

In 1936 he enrolled at the Art Students League in downtown Manhattan. There, he planned to pursue drawing, especially the drawing of political cartoons. But his teacher, George Grosz, who had left Germany to come to the United States, persuaded him to study realistic drawing and composition. Under Grosz, Bearden discovered the great Dutch painters as well as German and French artists. But he left the Art Students League after about a year and a half. He was anxious to be on his own and not to be dependent on his parents.

He got a job as a caseworker with the New York City Department of Welfare, and as soon as he had saved up enough money he moved into a studio apartment at 33 West 125th Street. The painter Jacob Lawrence had a studio on the floor below him, and soon a young poet named Claude McKay also moved into the building.

It was a wonderful time to be young and creative in Harlem. "There was a great interchange of people coming to Harlem from all over," Bearden recalled. "You got to know all kinds of people — actors, musicians, underworld characters, intellectuals, society types . . . There was always a lot of movement from place to place, and it was so easy to know people."

Through his friends, Bearden learned about art and all the different forms it could take. He went to his first exhibition of African art at the Museum of Modern Art, and what he saw gave him a great sense of pride in being black.

But Bearden was having difficulty deciding what to paint. At that time he was painting on brown paper, and he had a piece on his easel. But week after week he put nothing on the paper. One day the woman who cleaned for him once a week asked him if he wasn't supposed to be an artist. When he told her he was trying to decide what to paint, she suggested that he paint her. He looked at her. She said, "I know I'm homely, but when you can look at me and find what is beautiful, then you're going to be able to put something down on that piece of paper."

He thought about what she had said, and while he never did paint her, he did begin to paint. He started thinking about the summers he had spent as a child in Charlotte and painted pictures of his memories. He painted in bright colors and in a very stylized form. He didn't try to make the pictures look realistic, as most of his artist friends were doing. He exhibited several of his paintings at shows in Harlem and in one downtown gallery in 1940 and 1941.

In 1941 the United States entered World War II, and the following year Bearden went into the Army. The armed services were segregated in those days, and he served in the 372nd Infantry, a Negro regiment. He was stationed at various bases in the United States before being discharged in 1945 with the rank of sergeant.

Back in New York, Bearden moved into a studio on West 125th Street, next door to the famous Apollo Theatre, where all the major black entertainers performed. But he found that Harlem had changed. There had been riots in 1943, and people were no longer as friendly. Many of his artist friends had moved away, and the Harlem Artists Guild was no longer active. The more somber mood of Harlem seemed to fit the way Romare Bearden was feeling. His mother had died in 1943, and it took him a long time to get over the loss. He now made paintings using much less color and his figures were more realistic. He painted mostly religious subjects. He had several shows, but he still could not make a living as an artist.

In 1946 Bearden went back to work for the Department of Welfare. He painted at night. He still did not feel as if he had found the kinds of painting he wanted to do and worried that he had not had enough training. In 1949 he decided to go to Paris, where most of his artist friends had visited. He took a leave of absence from his job.

In Paris Bearden met the black American writers James Baldwin and Richard Wright. He also met the artists Picasso, Braque, and Brancusi. He did a lot of sightseeing but no painting. Instead, he soaked up ideas. He loved the city and applied for a scholarship to study there, but he did not get it and had to return to New York.

He went back to his job with the Department of Welfare and tried to figure out how he was going to save the money he needed to go back to Paris. He couldn't seem to make much of anything from his paintings, so he decided to write songs instead. A couple of his friends in the music business helped him, and before long he was writing song after song.

In two years, he had about twenty songs recorded, and one of them, "Seabreeze," was a big hit recorded by several popular singers. But Bearden didn't really want to be a songwriter. He wanted to be a painter. He was so unhappy that it began to affect him physically. He was sure he had some terrible disease and at one point went to the hospital. But doctors could find nothing physically wrong with him. The problem was in his mind. He was suffering from the pressure of doing what he didn't want to do and not doing what he *did* want to do. As one doctor told him, "You blew a fuse."

At that time Romare Bearden met Nanette Rohan at a party in Harlem. She was from Staten Island, New York, but her parents were from the West Indies. They fell in love and married soon afterward, and Bearden always credited Nanette Rohan with bringing him out of his unhappiness. Soon he was painting again.

But he still felt that he lacked training. He could not afford to go to Paris (in fact, for the first two years of their marriage, he and his new wife shared an apartment with his father on West 114th Street), so he started teaching himself by copying the great paintings of history. He would take a black-and-white photograph of a painting, have it blown up large, and then copy it, using his own color ideas. He became so interested in colors that when he did his own paintings, he painted in the abstract style, not concentrating on figures at all.

In 1956 Romare and Nanette Bearden moved out of Harlem and into a loft on Canal Street. A year or so after that he met a Chinese man named Mr. Wu who was an expert in Chinese art and calligraphy. With Mr. Wu's help, he began studying Chinese landscape paintings and learning that the spaces between shapes and colors can be as important as the shapes and colors themselves. He started painting on rice paper, gluing it to the canvas, and then tearing away sections.

Bearden was producing some wonderful work, but he found it very hard to find galleries interested in showing it. Even so, he was much better off than many other black artists, who couldn't get their work shown at all. More and more galleries were opening up in New York, and Bearden and his friends could not understand why there wasn't more interest in their work.

By this time, the early 1960s, the civil rights movement was in full swing. Blacks in the South were demanding the right to vote and to use public facilities equally with whites. Northern blacks like Bearden and his friends began to think about how discrimination could take many forms. In their case, they believed that black artists were discriminated against in the art world. White gallery owners and museum curators refused to look at their work purely as art. Rather, they saw it as art *by blacks* and dismissed it.

In 1963 a group of artists met in Bearden's loft and founded the Spiral Group, choosing that name because it meant to move up and out. They rented a room nearby where they met once a week and where they planned to put on exhibitions.

At one meeting, someone suggested that they work together on a painting. Bearden started thinking about how this would work, since they all had very different styles. Then it occurred to him that they could work together on a collage.

A collage is a combination of fragments, at least some of which are pasted on canvas or paper. It can be a combination of paper, or of paper and paint, or of paper, paint, and objects. Bearden decided to use pictures from magazines. He cut out a number of pictures and took them to the next meeting of the Spiral Group, but nobody else seemed very interested in his idea.

Still, he was interested enough to start working with the pictures. He pasted them on typewriter paper and then added watercolor paint and drawings. For his subjects, he called upon his many experiences and the many images that had impressed him — jazz music, African art, scenes from the South, Chinese landscapes, faces of people in Harlem. A friend suggested that he have them photographed and the photos blown up large. Bearden wasn't especially impressed with the result. But a gallery owner named Arne Ekstrom was. Bearden and Ekstrom decided to call the works "projections," and that was the name of the Bearden show that opened at the Cordier & Ekstrom Gallery in the fall of 1964.

The show was a great success and brought Bearden the most publicity he had ever enjoyed. He and his works were the subject of articles and mentions in *Time* and *Newsweek* magazines and in *The New York Times* as well as in many art magazines. Wrote the reviewer in *Pictures on Exhibit*, "Only a painter of rare sensitivity to tone and form could have worked out the patterns so eloquently, and only a deeply sentient person could have absorbed into his own emotional reservoir this travail of a whole people."

But Bearden was still not satisfied. He believed that photographs of his work removed it too far from the viewer. So he started gluing his photographs first to canvas, which warped, and then to wood, which did not warp. He worked with colors. The results were so successful that by 1966 he was finally making enough money as an artist to quit his job at the Department of Welfare.

Over the next twenty years Romare Bearden became a celebrated artist. Major museums bought his collages, and in 1971 the Museum of Modern Art in New York put on a whole show of his works from the beginning of his career. But like lesser-known artists who happened to be black, he never managed to achieve celebrity as an American artist without reference to his race. He was always called a black artist.

True, Bearden's themes were mainly about black life, but that was because he worked with subjects he knew best. His desire was to transcend or go beyond his subject matter and offer a vision of human life. But few critics, gallery owners, museum directors, and private collectors could understand that.

Most living black artists were nearly unknown, and it was much harder for a young black artist to find a gallery willing to show his work than it was for a young white artist. So in 1969 Bearden and two other artists opened the Cinqué Gallery to show the work of young black artists. Named after Joseph Cinqué, an African prince who led a successful revolt aboard a slave ship in 1839, the gallery later showed the work of older black artists and other minority artists who could not get shows at other galleries.

Romare Bearden also spent a great deal of time encouraging and helping young black artists on an informal basis. His telephone rang all the time, and he was happy to give advice whenever he could, even though he often had to interrupt his own work to do so.

He continued to work almost entirely in collage. No longer did he feel the need to try one form after another in order to find what he could do best. But within the collage form, he continued to experiment, always looking for a new way to place colors and shapes to offer his vision of life. Over the years he completely replaced the magazine and newspaper cutouts he had been using with bits of cut-up and repainted colored paper. Bearden's designs became more sophisticated, his colors richer and purer.

One thing that did not change was his subject matter. He continued to take from his own experiences, and that meant from black life.

He also continued to feel, and to say, that there was no such thing as "black art," just as there was no such thing as "white art." In 1946 he wrote, ". . . The true artist feels that there is only one art, and that it belongs to all mankind." Forty years later, he still felt that way.

In the last ten years of his life, Romare Bearden branched out into different types of art. He designed sets for the Alvin Ailey Dance Company and drew a backdrop for a Hollywood movie. The city of Baltimore asked him to design a mosaic mural for one of its subway stations. He illustrated a children's book entitled *A Trip to the Country*.

In 1988 Romare Bearden was given the National Medal of Arts by President Ronald Reagan. It was just one of many honors he received in his older years.

Bearden died of bone cancer in March 1988 at the age of seventy-five. In his will he directed that some of the money in his estate be used to set up the Romare Bearden Foundation to "aid, encourage and foster the education and training of deserving and talented art students."

8
Fannie Lou Hamer

When people think of the civil rights movement of the 1960s, they often think first of the educated male leaders such as Martin Luther King, Jr. But some of the most important work was done by poor, uneducated women. Fannie Lou Hamer reached national fame through her courage and determination to fight for basic civil rights.

She was born Fannie Lou Townsend in 1917 in Montgomery County, Mississippi. She was the granddaughter of a slave, and although slavery had been abolished for more than fifty years, her family lived just one step above slavery. Her parents were sharecroppers. They farmed a plot of land on the plantation for the plantation owner, who received a percentage of the crops harvested. The rest they kept for themselves. But the house they lived in belonged to the plantation. They bought their seed and other supplies from the plantation, as well as the food they could not grow themselves, like coffee and flour and sugar. By the time they finished paying the owner for all that, there was little left over for them.

What they did manage to keep for themselves had to be stretched very far. Fannie Lou was the last of twenty children in a family of six girls and fourteen boys. Although as the baby of the family she was very much loved, she did not have a happy childhood. She contracted polio when she was young. There was no vaccine for polio in those days, and her family had no money for doctors. She survived the disease, but it left her with a limp.

The limp, and her short stature, did not prevent her from "standing tall" as a person. One thing her mother taught her at an early age was to "stand up no matter what the odds." She went to work in the fields at the age of six. Large-boned and sturdily built, she proved to be a strong worker.

Fannie once said, "I can remember very well the landowner telling me one day that if I would pick thirty pounds he would give me something out of the commissary: some Cracker-Jacks, Daddy Wide-Legs, and some sardines. These were things that he knew I loved and never had a chance to have. So I picked thirty pounds that day. Well, the next week I had to pick sixty and by the time I was thirteen I was picking two and three hundred pounds."

It was backbreaking work, for picking cotton meant cleaning each cotton plant of its ripe bolls, starting from the top and working down. Dragging a long bag behind her, Fannie moved slowly along a row, not even noticing the nicks and cuts in her toughened hands caused by the sharp edges of the outer casing of the boll.

But Fannie and all the other children had to work to help out the family. Her parents once tried to farm for themselves, but a white man killed all their mules and they had to go back to sharecropping. Fannie had little schooling. "My parents tried so hard to do what they could to keep us in school, but school [for black children] didn't last but four months out of the year and most of the time we didn't have clothes to wear. I dropped out of school and cut cornstalks to help the family."

Fannie got married in 1944 at the age of twenty-seven to Perry Hamer, whom she called "Pap." She moved in with him at the Marlow plantation in Ruleville, Mississippi, where he had lived for twelve years. As sharecroppers on that plantation, the Hamers were given a "furnish," a small house, and credit against their work at the plantation store. Despite Hamer's lack of schooling, she was smart and a trustworthy worker. Eventually she became the plantation timekeeper, keeping track of the hours each worker put in, and letting the other workers know when it was time to take a break, when it was time to return to work, and when it was quitting time.

Hamer interrupted her work only twice — to have children. The local white doctor did not believe that black women should have a lot of children, and he took it upon himself to sterilize Fannie. Fannie did not realize at the time that the surgery he performed meant that she could never have another child. By the time she did realize what he had done, it was too late. People who knew and worked with her in later years described her as having large, sad eyes. A lot happened to her in her life to be sad about.

In spite of all the hardships she endured, Fannie Lou Hamer had a strong sense of her own self-worth. She was proud of her ability to work hard and felt she was just as good as the next person, black or white. She resented the segregation under which she had lived all her life and felt she was entitled to all the rights of citizenship. As she put it, "I just knowed things wasn't right."

In 1975 she recalled the time when she and her family had moved into a house on the Marlow plantation that had previously been lived in by a white family. The house had a bathroom, but it wasn't working. When she asked that it be fixed, Marlow told her she didn't need it. "And several weeks after that," said Hamer, "I was over to they house cleaning up a bathroom, and his daughter told me — she was a little girl then — she told me I didn't have to take too much pains in that room, because that was old Honey's bathroom, and that was they dog.

"I was mad enough to boil when I left that

house . . . and I went home and I told Pap, I said, 'Now they got they dog higher'n us.' "

Hamer did not keep her feelings to herself, but talked freely in the fields about the conditions under which she and the other workers lived. Since that kind of talk was dangerous, some of the others said she didn't have good sense. But for many years she did not know how to do more than talk. She had no idea how to fight for her rights. She was no different from most black people in the South.

The U.S. political system allows people to make changes through voting. But in the South the system for voting was controlled by whites, who passed laws making it nearly impossible for blacks to register. For many years, black people could not register to vote unless they had a white person to vouch for them. Few whites were willing to vouch for blacks, since they did not want them to have the vote. That law was struck down in the 1940s. But whites came up with other ways to keep blacks from getting the vote. They started requiring a written test, knowing that many blacks could not read or write well enough to pass it. Sometimes even a black person who passed the test was told that he or she had not. Those who passed the test then had to pay poll taxes back to the time they were twenty-one years old, which a lot of black people could not afford.

There were many other indignities, like segregated schools and segregated buses. In the mid-1950s in Montgomery, the capital of Alabama,

blacks were especially angered over their treat-
ment on the segregated buses. They could only
sit in the back of the bus, and when the bus became crowded, they had to give up even the back
seats to whites who were standing. In 1955 a
seamstress in Montgomery named Rosa Parks refused to give up her bus seat to a white man and
was arrested. Her arrest sparked a black boycott
of the Montgomery buses.

A young Baptist minister named Martin Luther
King, Jr., emerged as a leader of the boycott,
which was finally successful after more than a
year. The United States Supreme Court ruled that
segregation of the buses was unconstitutional.
Martin Luther King, Jr., and other southern
ministers believed that they could win more bat-
tles against segregation through boycotts and
other forms of nonviolent protest. They formed
the Southern Christian Leadership Conference
(SCLC) to work for change in the South.

Not long afterward, in 1960, black college students in Greensboro, North Carolina, began their
own nonviolent campaign against segregation at
lunch counters in the city. The form of protest
they chose was a sit-in: They sat at the lunch
counters until they were served, or arrested and
taken away by the police. Other college students
did the same thing, and soon they formed the
Student Nonviolent Coordinating Committee
(SNCC).

Both SCLC and SNCC believed that if blacks
could vote, they could bring about more changes.

Both launched voter-registration drives in different parts of the South. SCLC concentrated on Alabama. SNCC chose Mississippi as the focus of its campaign.

Fannie Lou Hamer had been following the progress of what was now being called the civil rights movement. When young SNCC workers came to Ruleville to try to get local blacks to register to vote, she was willing to try, even though she knew it meant great danger. She was then forty-four years old and had worked on the Marlow plantation for eighteen years.

As she explained later, "One day in early August, I heard that some young people had come to town teaching people how to register to vote. I have always wanted to do something to help myself and my race, but I did not know how to go about it. So, I went to one of the meetings in Ruleville. That night, I was showed how to fill out a form for registration. The next day, August 31, 1962, I went to Indianola, Mississippi, to fill out a form at the registrar's office. I took the test."

The registrar gave Hamer a book containing the Mississippi Constitution and told her to copy the sixteenth section of it. She copied it. Then he asked her to tell him what it meant. She flunked.

That night when she returned home, she learned that Marlow, the landowner, had been telling everybody in the field what would happen if she tried to register again.

"That night, Marlow came to the house where I was staying, and called Mr. Hamer to the door.

I could hear him telling my husband what he was going to do to me if I did not withdraw my registration, so I went to the door. Marlow asked my husband if he had told me what he had said. Marlow saw me in the door and asked me why I went to register. I told him that I did it for myself, not for him. He told me to get off the plantation and don't be seen near it again. That night I left the plantation and went to stay with Mr. and Mrs. Tucker in Ruleville." Her husband had to remain on the plantation until the work was done.

Whites were prepared to use any means necessary to keep blacks from voting. On September 10, 1962, night riders fired sixteen shots into the Tuckers' house. Fortunately for Hamer, she was not in the house that night, for shots hit the bedroom wall one foot above where her head normally rested.

She would not be frightened off. In early December she found a three-room house to rent, and she and her family moved into it. The next day she went back to try again to register to vote. She had studied the Mississippi Constitution and this time was able to interpret the section given to her.

Now that she had registered to vote, she wanted others to do the same. She agreed to work with SNCC, and she became one of their most energetic field secretaries, traveling across the South.

On June 9, 1963, she and five other SNCC and SCLC workers were returning by bus to Greenwood, Mississippi, from a meeting in South Carolina. When the bus stopped in Winona, Mississippi, some of the workers went into the white waiting room. Hamer was not one of them. The local police arrived and arrested the whole group, including Fannie Lou Hamer, who had just stepped off the bus to see what was going on.

At the Winona jail they were all placed in one cell at first. Then a young woman named Annelle Ponder, an SCLC voter-education teacher who was stationed in Mississippi, was taken from the cell. The others heard her screaming and realized that she was being beaten. Hamer remembered hearing Annelle screaming and crying, and at the same time praying out loud for God to forgive the men who were beating her.

Then Hamer was taken from the cell and brought to another cell. Three white men and two black prisoners were there. A white man handed a blackjack to one of the prisoners and ordered him to make Hamer "wish she was dead." While a white man held her down, the prisoner beat her all over her body. Then the other prisoner took over with the blackjack. Hamer tried to protect her head with her hands. She was beaten until her fingers were blue. The skin of her back swelled up and turned hard with welts. When the beating was finished, Hamer could not even walk.

Other SNCC staff arrived in Winona and paid the bail for Hamer and the others. SNCC lawyers filed suit against the Winona police for the arrests and beatings. The case came to trial the following December. Hamer and the other SNCC workers testified about what had happened. The white owner of the restaurant at the bus stop and the white waitress who had been there the night of the arrests both testified. So did the two black prisoners. An FBI agent who had taken pictures of Hamer and the others after they had been beaten showed those pictures to the court. But in spite of all the evidence against them, all the whites who had been charged were found not guilty.

The verdict did not surprise Hamer. It was the same southern justice she had known her whole life. But it just made her more determined to bring about change in Mississippi.

She remained based in Ruleville, although she often traveled to other cities and towns. In March 1964 a friend who was still working on the Marlow plantation warned her that he'd heard someone say, "Mrs. Hamer thinks she is a big woman now but she'll be killed." This was not the only threat she had received against her life. But she didn't back down. In fact, she was one of the most determined SNCC workers.

She would often wake everyone else up by saying, "I'm sick and tired of being sick and tired." Whenever something happened that moved her, she would stand up and sing her favorite spiritual, "This little light of mine, I'm gonna let it shine." The other SNCC workers, who were mostly college students or college graduates, and who were both black and white, found her to be a natural leader, in spite of her lack of education. As one white female SNCC worker put it, "Mrs. Hamer is more educated than I am. That is, she knows more."

She was never afraid to speak her mind. One time, a group in Illinois that was sympathetic to the civil rights movement and the poor people of Mississippi sent a truckload of clothing. Hamer made plans to distribute it. On that day, the mayor of Ruleville announced on the radio that clothing was being given away and where to go to get it. His plan was that a large crowd would gather and become unruly, making Mrs. Hamer and SNCC look as if they couldn't organize even a simple clothing distribution.

Sure enough, a large crowd gathered. Worried, Fannie Hamer called the local SNCC office and asked what she should do and was told to handle the situation as best she could. She walked over to the crowd and said, "The mayor can't tell Negroes what to do. If you all would just go down to the courthouse to register to vote, we wouldn't have a mayor doing things like this to us." She managed to calm the crowd and distribute the clothing in an orderly way.

Nineteen sixty-four was an election year in Mississippi. All the candidates on the ballot were white. The SNCC voting rights workers decided to put up four local black leaders as write-in candidates. Voters could write these names on the ballots instead of voting for any of the official candidates. No one expected the write-in candidates to win, but SNCC felt it was a way to get publicity for their cause.

Fannie Hamer agreed to be a write-in candidate. She spent most of the late winter and spring attending meetings in different parts of the county, urging black people to register and to vote for her. After the June 2 primary, which of course none of the black candidates won, she and several voters tried to attend a local precinct meeting of the Democratic party. They found the door locked. They were not surprised. SNCC had already decided to form its own Mississippi Freedom Democratic Party (MFDP).

SNCC declared that summer to be Mississippi Freedom Summer and that it would do everything possible to get blacks registered. More than a thousand volunteers, many white and many from the North, arrived in Mississippi to work in the campaign. In June two young white men named Andrew Goodman and Michael Schwerner arrived in Mississippi and were picked up by a local black civil rights worker named James Chaney. He was to drive them to SNCC headquarters. The three were murdered by local whites, and their bodies buried in the side of a dam in Meridien, Mississippi.

At the Democratic national convention in Atlantic City that August, Fannie Hamer and other MFDP delegates attempted to challenge the regular Mississippi delegation as not being representative of the people of Mississippi. Several other state delegations supported their challenge. Fannie Hamer made a speech before the Credentials Committee, saying, "If the Freedom Democratic Party is not seated now, I question America. Is this America? The land of the free and the home of the brave? Where we have to sleep with our telephones off the hook, because our lives be threatened daily?" She told how blacks in Mississippi were prevented from voting, from attending precinct meetings, from the most basic forms of democracy. She told about how she had been beaten in Winona the year before. Then she broke down and wept.

National Democratic leaders offered a compromise. They would give the MFDP two seats, and promised that from then on, the regular Mississippi delegation would never again be all-white. But Hamer would not accept the compromise. Martin Luther King, Jr., urged her to change her mind. So did many other leaders, black and white. But she refused. The regular Mississippi delegation was seated. No MFDP delegates were officially recognized at the convention.

That fall, Hamer led an MFDP challenge to the seating of the Mississippi Congressional Delegation when the new session of Congress opened. Once again they were not successful. But with each challenge, they caused more people to think about how much the southern states had excluded blacks from participating as equal citizens. In 1965 Congress passed, and President Lyndon B. Johnson signed, the Voting Rights Act that empowered federal registrars to register black votes in the South. Fannie Hamer and the others in the MFDP believed their work had helped bring about the new law.

In September 1964 Mrs. Hamer and a group of other SNCC workers went to Guinea, the second African nation to become independent, as guests of the government. For Hamer, who had not even traveled outside of Mississippi very often, it was an exciting experience.

"Being from the South we never was taught much about our African heritage," wrote Hamer in her autobiography, *To Praise Our Bridges*. "The way everybody talked to us, everybody in Africa was savages and really stupid people. But I've seen more savage white folks here in America than I seen in Africa. I saw black men flying the airplanes, driving buses, sitting behind the big desks in the bank and just doing everything that I was used to seeing white people do. I saw, for the first time in my life, a black stewardess walking through the plane and that was quite an inspiration for me."

But rapid change was coming to the American South. By the following year *Mississippi* magazine had named Fannie Lou Hamer one of six "Women of Influence" in the state. In the early 1970s Ruleville held a Fannie Lou Hamer Day, and the white mayor said she would go down in history as a champion of her people. By 1975 representatives of white candidates were visiting her at the small brick house where she and Pap lived in Ruleville to ask for her support.

That winter, Hamer's health began to fail, but she worked hard in 1976 to unite the black and white factions of the Mississippi Democratic party so that a single integrated delegation could represent the state at the 1976 Democratic national convention in New York. She died of cancer on March 15, 1977, at the age of sixty.

At her funeral, Andrew Young, a leader in the SCLC who would later become U.S. Ambassador to the United Nations and Mayor of Atlanta, Georgia, said, "Women were the spine of our movement. It was women going door-to-door, speaking with their neighbors, meeting in voter-registration classes together, organizing through their churches, that gave the vital momentum and energy to the movement. Mrs. Hamer was special but she was also representative."

The stout woman with the limp and the big, sad eyes, who lacked an education and had experienced so much pain in her life, would not have wanted to be remembered as either special or representative. She would have wanted to be remembered simply as someone who had known things weren't right and who had done her best to do something about it.

9
Eddie Robinson

In 1986 Eddie Robinson, football coach at Grambling State University in Louisiana, became the "winningest" football coach (professional as well as collegiate) in history when his Grambling State University Tigers beat the Prairie View A&M Panthers at the Cotton Bowl in Dallas. The 27–7 win brought his career won-lost-tied record to 324–106–15. With that win, Robinson broke the record of the legendary University of Alabama coach, Bear Bryant, who had retired. Since Robinson himself was only sixty-six and had several more years to go before retirement, he had the opportunity to rack up many more wins and set a record not likely to be broken by any other coach in the foreseeable future. What's more, Eddie Robinson would retire having won all his games at a single school, a record that will probably never be broken.

That particular record is due not just to the fact that Eddie Robinson never seriously considered leaving Grambling since he was offered his first coaching job there at the age of twenty-two. It is also due to the fact of segregation. When Robinson was hired at Grambling, the only jobs available to him as a coach were at black schools, just as the only schools that had been available to him as a student had been segregated ones.

Edward Gay Robinson was born on February 12, 1919, in Jackson, Louisiana, a small farming community outside of Baton Rouge where three generations of his family had been sharecroppers. His parents were poor, hardworking people who wanted to better themselves. When Eddie was still young, his father went to Baton Rouge to look for a non-farm job. Eddie and his mother remained in Jackson, and Eddie was raised in his grandparents' house. He grew very close to his grandfather, who taught him, "There's no work too hard if it gets you what you need or where you want to go."

As a youngster Eddie helped out with the farm work as soon as he was old enough to do so. When he was eight he and his mother joined his father in Baton Rouge, where Frank Robinson had found a steady job with Standard Oil Company. Two years later, his parents divorced. His mother found jobs as a housekeeper, and Eddie divided his time between his mother's and father's homes.

In Baton Rouge, Eddie was able to go to school more than four months out of the year. But he continued to work. Over the years he picked strawberries, shined shoes, and delivered newspapers to help out his mother. He also found time to play sports. After school he and his friends played football. They didn't have a real football, so they used a blown-up pig's bladder. Unfortunately, this did not prepare them very well to play with a real football, and when they got a chance to play against a team across town that did have a real ball, they were badly beaten. Fortunately, a player on a nearby white high school football team took an interest in them. He taught them how to block and tackle, and the next time they played the team across town they won.

Eddie attended McKinley High School, which to his great delight had a football team. He starred at tailback but played other positions as well. He also met fellow student Doris Mott when both were thirteen. They were sweethearts all through high school and planned to marry after they finished college.

Eddie's high school football career earned him a partial scholarship as a player-coach at Leland College, a Baptist school in Baker, Louisiana. He went on recruiting trips with the coach, Reuben S. Turner, and was often left in charge of practice. On the team, he was a single-wing tailback, fullback, punter, and passer. The scholarship was not

enough to cover all his college expenses, so Eddie also worked on a coal truck for twenty cents an hour, and worked as the campus barber. An English major, he especially liked British eighteenth- and nineteenth-century poets and even today will quote extensively from Rudyard Kipling and Henry Wadsworth Longfellow.

After graduation in 1941, Eddie and Doris were married, and Eddie went to work tossing grain in a Baton Rouge feed mill for twenty-five cents an hour. Soon they were expecting their first child, and so Eddie took a second job evenings unloading blocks of ice from a mule-drawn wagon and delivering them to the kitchens of private homes. There were few jobs available to a black man with a college degree, especially the kind of job Eddie wanted, which was coaching. Fortunately, someone in Doris's family knew Ralph Waldo Emerson Jones, president of Louisiana Negro Normal and Industrial Institute in Grambling, Louisiana, about sixty miles from Shreveport. Through his family connections, Eddie arranged to have an interview.

Founded in 1901 as the Colored Industrial and Agricultural School, the school consisted of eight buildings and had an enrollment of 320. There was no athletic department. But President Jones had big hopes for the school. He wanted it to become a full-fledged university, and he was looking for a young man who could establish its first athletic department.

Years later, Robinson recalled that interview: "The talk rambled to baseball and I admitted I was one heck of a hitter. Dr. Jones said he was the best pitcher these parts had ever seen. I said I could hit any pitcher I faced. He said, 'Let's get a mitt and we'll *see.*' We went outside. His brief warm-up told me the man could *throw.* But I could *hit.* Suddenly I remembered it was a job I was after. I went down swinging on three straight pitches — and got the job."

At age twenty-two Robinson was probably the youngest college coach in America. He was without a doubt the busiest. As a one-man athletic department, he coached not just football but also baseball and both men's and women's basketball. His one assistant was the school's night watchman. Robinson mowed the football field, sewed torn uniforms, and taped the players' ankles. He drilled the cheerleaders, directed the band, and even wrote the game accounts for the local newspapers. His budget was $64.00 a year. His salary was not much larger. The job did come with a place to live, and Eddie and Doris Robinson moved into an old, weatherbeaten house with no electricity, running water, or indoor toilet.

Coach Robinson's first year at the college was not memorable. The team posted a 3–5 record, playing home games on a field that had no bleachers, so fans had to stand. The cheerleaders had a hard time coming up with cheers using the school's long and rather awkward name. Recalled

Robinson, "Used to be when the other team was down at our goal line, our students would yell: 'Hold that line Louisiana Negro Normal and Industrial Institute!' Before they could finish the cheer, the other guys would score." Everyone was grateful when Dr. Jones changed the name of the school to Grambling College in 1946 (it became Grambling State University in 1974).

By the 1942 season Eddie Robinson had had a chance to shape up his football team. He had also started an ambitious recruiting drive, traveling to black high schools across the state to watch games and invite players he was interested in to attend Grambling. He couldn't offer them much in the way of scholarships, but he could promise them a good education and excellent training in football. From the start, he stressed that his athletes be well-rounded young men who paid attention to their schoolwork and did not miss classes. Every weekday morning at six o'clock he roused his athletes with an old wooden-handled school bell to make sure they ate a proper breakfast and got to their early classes on time. Grambling had a record of 9–0 in Robinson's second year.

In the early years the football seasons were short. College football was as segregated as other areas of American life, and black teams could play only other black teams. Eddie Robinson groomed his athletes as if they would be playing against the top teams in college football, and as the years wore on he was certain they could hold their own against any team. They just never got a chance to prove it.

Sometimes it was hard to motivate his athletes, for there were no opportunities for them to play football after college. Professional football was still pretty much closed to blacks, and until 1949 no football player from a black college had ever made it to the National Football League.

In the late 1940s Paul "Tank" Younger, Grambling's star fullback, piled up sixty touchdowns for the Tigers. Grambling was still pretty much unknown at that time, but a scout for the Los Angeles Rams heard about Younger and came to Grambling to see him. The scout was impressed but concerned about Younger's ability to perform in the NFL, which, he reminded Robinson, had never before signed a player from a black school. Coach Robinson told the scout that Younger was not a *black* fullback but an *American* fullback and was better than any fullback from the bigger colleges. The Rams took a chance and signed Younger for top rookie pay. Younger went on to compile a distinguished record in the pros and today is assistant general manager of the San Diego Chargers. Says he of Robinson, "Eddie had a game plan for your life, not just a Saturday."

Once Younger showed what kind of quality football players Grambling was capable of turning out, the ice was broken in the NFL. Since 1949

Robinson has sent more than 200 players into the National Football League. He also sent a number of players to the short-lived United States Football League (USFL).

The reluctance of the pro leagues was not the only type of discrimination Eddie Robinson and his team had to contend with in the early days. They also faced a good many problems on the road. Allowed to play only teams from other black colleges, the team was required to travel by bus across the South, and in the 1940s, '50s, and early '60s, that meant meeting segregation at every turn. Once they boarded the rickety old team bus, which was nicknamed Blue Bird, they had to drive until they reached their destination. No white restaurants along the way would serve them, unless they were willing to get takeout food from the back door. White service stations would allow the bus to fill up with gas, but would not allow the players to use the bathrooms.

Sometimes when traveling, the team was even unable to find a field on which to practice. That happened once in Montgomery, Alabama, where the opposing team, Alabama State, did not have its own football field and instead used a town field. Denied the use of the football field to work out on the day before the game, Eddie Robinson had the bus stop in an empty parking lot and held practice there.

Conditions were not much better on the Grambling campus, where there was no money to plant new grass on the football field. For years, the Tigers practiced and played on dirt.

In spite of these hardships the Grambling football team thrived — and not just as players, but as young men. Early on, Robinson established the tradition that incoming freshmen had to give a speech to the team about where they came from and something about their background. Very few were skilled at public speaking, and so Coach Robinson asked for, and got, a special course in social etiquette. Not only did this course teach his players how to speak properly, but it also taught them how to shake hands, how to enter and leave a room, and how to hold a knife and fork properly. He insisted that his players wear coats and ties to away games. He always wore a coat and tie to games both at home and away. In the days when Grambling games were not covered in the national press and Grambling players had little reason to be poised and articulate for reporters, Eddie Robinson had them prepared to give interviews in front of a national audience. He often said, "I want to see to it that every guy gets the opportunity to be the best man he can be."

He was like a father to his players. They came to him with their family and romance problems, and he always had the time to listen to them and offer advice. Many credit him with whatever success they have achieved in life, whether in football or in other areas. Some went on to careers in law and medicine and other professions and attributed their success to Robinson's stress on the basics of discipline and hard work. It is to Robinson's credit that more than eighty percent of Grambling players have graduated, a much higher percentage than at most colleges.

Each fall, it became the custom for players who had graduated to return to Grambling to help Coach Robinson in preseason practice. Others kept in touch through phone calls and letters and frequent visits. While Robinson had two children of his own, a son and a daughter, at times it seemed as if he had hundreds of other sons as well.

Robinson's former players considered themselves a special group, and the mystique of playing at Grambling, although confined mostly to the southern black community, was important to the coach's recruiting. This was especially important after the civil rights movement began to open up more opportunities for blacks to go to college. A variety of legal suits against segregated higher education in the South forced southern state universities to admit black students. Colleges in the North also started recruiting more black athletes. All of these colleges and universities had more scholarship money and better athletic facilities to offer than did Grambling. Eddie Robinson realized the school had to change with the times.

Eddie Robinson had always been flexible and

willing to make changes when they were needed. The idea that a man who stays in the same job year after year gets stuck in his ways and doesn't have imagination does not hold in the case of Robinson. From the first he was willing to change his plays on the field when necessary, with the result that both his offensive and defensive arsenals were huge. His players were prepared to change tactics at a moment's notice, making them more flexible than many other teams.

He also introduced innovations on the field. In the old days, the players were not given drinking water during a game. Robinson introduced drinking water onto the field before other coaches did. Now, water is always available to football players during a game.

When he saw that changing racial and social conditions were opening up more opportunities for black athletes, Robinson decided that Grambling's athletic program had to change its focus and think bigger than it ever had before. In 1965, with President Jones and Collie J. Nicholson, Grambling's publicist, he took a long, hard look at Grambling. The college was still so small that it did not have a large alumni base to give it money. It still lacked a decent home stadium. To overcome these obstacles, the three decided that Grambling had to have a *national* black collegiate team. Only in this way could it attract the publicity and support needed to keep top high school players coming and to raise the money for better athletic facilities.

Nicholson started sending out press releases about the team twice a week to national newspapers and magazines. President Jones and Coach Robinson put out the word that the Tigers were interested in playing exhibition games in big stadiums. They got their first big exhibition game in 1968. On September 28, in Yankee Stadium in New York, the Grambling Tigers played Morgan State of Baltimore, Maryland, in front of more than 60,000 fans, most of them black. Grambling lost 9–7, but they were proud of the way they played and pleased with the chance to show what they could do.

Over the next few years, the team played in Los Angeles, Cleveland, Detroit, Pittsburgh, Chicago, Houston, Dallas, Kansas City, and other major cities, each time to huge, predominantly black crowds.

The team made money from these games and used it to increase the entertainment value of the games. Grambling's band became a marvel of intricate, synchronized movements, and the halftime show became worthy of attendance itself. Television networks started picking up the games, bringing in more revenue and more publicity for Grambling. Eddie Robinson called the Tigers "a gypsy team with a floating schedule," willing to play anybody anywhere if the terms were right. Some observers likened the Tigers to the Harlem Globetrotters basketball team, which plays exhibition games around the world. Grambling reached international status in 1976 when the team and the band visited Japan and played an exhibition game against Morgan State.

But perhaps a bigger milestone for Robinson had come two years earlier, when the team had played a regular-season game in the Sugar Bowl in New Orleans. Robinson remarked at the time that the event meant a lot more to him than it did to the players because he remembered a time when blacks could not even sit in the Sugar Bowl, let alone play in it.

With national renown came talk that Eddie Robinson might be recruited to coach at a larger school or even in the pros. But Robinson had no interest in going elsewhere and never seriously entertained any outside offers. He realized he could make more money elsewhere, and he would have enjoyed having extra money for recruiting players. But in the end he felt he owed his success to Grambling and could not imagine leaving either it or the team.

Robinson's loyalty to the Grambling Tigers was echoed in the loyalty of black football players to the school. Although the Tigers had a white backup quarterback named James Gregory in 1968 (whose story inspired a TV movie entitled *Grambling's White Tiger*), and the school has a small percentage of white students, it remains predominantly black. It still attracts some of the best high school players, some of whom turn down lucrative scholarship offers from big schools in favor of Grambling.

While the Grambling teams of the 1960s are judged to have been the best in the school's history — in 1960 the defensive team featured four All-Pros — Grambling had more winning teams since integration began than during the era of segregation. According to *Sports Illustrated* magazine, from 1953 to 1972 the Tigers won seventy-three percent of their games, while between 1973 and 1982 they won almost eighty percent. More than anything else, this success was due to Eddie Robinson.

By 1982, after forty-one years at Grambling, Coach Robinson was approaching the kinds of records that have been won by only a few great coaches. In late September an upcoming game against Florida A&M, a predominantly black college, loomed as his 300th win. The Florida fans at Bragg Memorial Stadium chanted, "Not in Tallahassee, Eddie. NOT IN TALLAHASSEE!" The game was tied 14–14 at halftime, and by the beginning of the fourth quarter the Tigers had fallen behind 21–14. The team was worried, but not the coach. "All we have to do is throw shorter," he said, and in the next five minutes wingback Trumaine Johnson scored three times, leading the Tigers, with a 3–0 season record, to a 43–21 win for their coach.

Without shame, Eddie Robinson cried. "I'm a crier," he explained. "I can't hold it back. I owe so much to so many. We came back, showed the character you need in life. With work you can make outstanding people out of ordinary guys."

With that win, Robinson joined a very exclusive club as the fourth coach in history to have 300 or more wins. Still ahead of him were Bear Bryant of the University of Alabama with 318, Amos Alonzo Stagg of the University of Chicago with 314, and Glen Scobie "Pop" Warner, who had coached at seven colleges, with 313. Robinson was not only the one member of the "300 Club" who had earned all his victories at one college, he was also the only black in the club. Bear Bryant was due to retire soon, and since Robinson was just sixty-three, there was every reason to believe that he would surpass them all. That put a lot of pressure on Eddie Robinson.

He did his best not to let that pressure affect him. A few years earlier, he had let winning become too important. He had taken losing too hard. Finally his wife, Doris, had suggested that if he didn't cool it, he would have a heart attack. He calmed down after that. Fortunately, there were far more wins than losses. At the end of the fall 1982 season, Grambling and Robinson could claim twenty-three straight winning seasons.

The following year, Grambling's brand-new campus stadium opened. A huge marker at the entrance proclaimed: ROBINSON STADIUM "WHERE EVERYBODY IS SOMEBODY." Its seating capacity was 27,000, and there were plans to expand that to 43,000 when additional money was raised.

Grambling now had a student population of 4,500, nearly every one of whom would be at the stadium for every game. The college, and the team, had come a long way since 1941. So had the state of Louisiana, which had paid the bulk of the $7.5 million cost of the new stadium.

But the South was still the South, and as Eddie Robinson approached Bear Bryant's record, much pressure was placed on him, including the questioning of his own early record at Grambling. Whenever a sports record is about to be broken, outside observers take sides. In no case is this more true than when a black threatens a record held by a white.

Some people began to question the records of the Tigers between 1941 and 1949, when Grambling did not keep careful statistics. A school with a one-man athletic department who mowed the grass and drew the white lines on the field was not going to be very careful about keeping athletic records. The problem was compounded by the fact that back in the early 1960s, Grambling's president, began joking that the Grambling Tigers in Robinson's first year had had a record of 0–8, while in the second season it was 9–0. Johnson was trying to make the coach's second-season record seem even more impressive. But Grambling press guides and sportswriters had picked up this quote and reported it. The National Collegiate Athletic Association (NCAA), however, insisted that the correct record was 3–5. Others complained that more than 300 of Robinson's victories had come against small-college teams, while Bryant's had come against big-school teams.

The two men themselves had nothing but respect for each other and had known one another for years. Back in his early days as a coach, Eddie Robinson had attended every Bear Bryant football clinic he could. In 1982 Bryant had presented Robinson with the Walter Camp Foundation's 1982 Distinguished American Award. When Bryant died in 1983, Robinson could not get a flight, so he drove 400 miles through the night to Tuscaloosa, Alabama, to attend the funeral. "I could win 1,000 games and never replace the Bear," he said.

His one regret was that his Grambling Tigers and the Crimson Tide of Alabama had never met on the field. What a match that would have been! But a small-college team like Grambling would never be matched up with a big-school team on a regular NCAA schedule. And no exhibition game between the schools was ever held, in large measure because of the racial issues involved.

By the fall of 1985 Eddie Robinson had matched Bear Bryant's final record of 323 wins. The upcoming game against Prairie View A&M on Saturday, October 12, could result in the magic win number 324. Although the potential for Bryant fans to be soreheaded was there,

Robinson did not receive a single hate letter.

Dozens of former Grambling players were at the Cotton Bowl for the big game, including Tank Younger, Hall of Famer Willie Davis, and Doug Williams, the most successful black quarterback in the history of the NFL. The president of Grambling at that time, Dr. Joseph B. Johnson, had years earlier been recruited for the football team by Robinson. They were not disappointed. Grambling scored on its first and third possessions to go ahead 14–0 and by halftime had a 20–0 lead. The final score was 27–7, a commanding 324th win for the winningest coach in football history.

Eddie Robinson cried after that game, too. "Let it out, coach!" shouted his players, and he did. But he insisted, "The *real* record is forty-four years at one school, one job and one wife."

The real record was also working within the system of segregation that was in place for so many of Coach Robinson's years at Grambling. "I grew up in the South," he said. "I was told where to attend elementary school, where to attend junior high school, where to attend high school. When I became a coach, I was told who I could recruit, who I could play, and when I could play. I did what I could within the system."

Asked how he wanted to be remembered, Robinson said, "I always knew my part to play, and if my part ended up having something to do with history, then I'm happy. I never let anybody change my faith in this country. All I want is for my story to be an American story, not black and not white. Just American. I want it to belong to everybody."

10
Shirley Chisholm

"**M**s. Chis for Pres" proclaimed the campaign buttons that women, and some men, proudly wore during the 1972 presidential primary election campaign. Today, those buttons are collectors' items, because they are artifacts of a special time in American history.

The term "Ms.," instead of Miss or Mrs., was just coming into use in 1972. It was a term used by and for women who did not feel their names should identify them as being married or not. After all, "Mr." could mean a married man or a bachelor. Why should women's titles be any different?

The early 1970s were the time of the feminist movement, when women demonstrated for rights they did not have. They wanted equal jobs for equal pay. They wanted the same rights as men had. They pushed for an Equal Rights Amendment to the United States Constitution.

Today, people feel comfortable using the term "Ms." Women work in jobs that were previously denied them and enjoy greater opportunities in many areas. Shirley Chisholm, a black woman, helped to bring those changes about. As a black person, she has suffered much discrimination in her life; but she says that she has often suffered more discrimination because she is a woman.

Shirley Chisholm did not win the Democratic party's nomination as its presidential candidate in 1972. But she won enough votes in the primaries to show that a black woman could be considered a serious candidate. She paved the way for Jesse Jackson to run for president, and for Geraldine Ferraro to run as the first woman vice-presidential candidate from a major political party (she ran with Walter Mondale in 1980). Chisholm has been a trailblazer in many ways.

Shirley Chisholm was born Shirley Ann St. Hill in Brooklyn, New York, in 1924. Her parents, Charles and Ruby St. Hill, were both from the West Indian island of Barbados, and both had immigrated to New York in the early 1920s seeking a better life. They had known each other slightly in Barbados, and were married soon after they met again in Brooklyn. Shirley was the first of their three daughters.

Like many other West Indian immigrants, Charles and Ruby St. Hill wanted to own a house and provide a good education for their children. But it was hard to realize their dreams. Charles

St. Hill had hoped to get a factory job, but the only work he could find was as a baker's helper. Ruby St. Hill was an excellent seamstress, but with three little girls to raise, she could not go out to work. She helped out with household expenses by taking in sewing. Little Shirley loved to play with her mother's sewing machine. When her mother tried to put it up out of reach, Shirley piled up chairs and climbed until she could get to it.

Shirley was a determined, independent little girl from an early age. By the time she was three years old, she was bossing her younger sisters, Odessa, age two, and the infant Muriel. Years later her mother told her that when she was three, she used to go up to the six- and seven-year-old kids in the neighborhood, punch them, and say, "Listen to me." What Chisholm likes to refer to as her "mouth" was becoming famous even then.

Shirley was fortunate to be so independent so young, because when she was still three years old she and her sisters were sent to Barbados to be cared for by their grandmother. Charles St. Hill could not support his family on his income as a baker's helper. Ruby St. Hill had to go out to work. It was her idea to take the girls to her mother, just for a few years, until she and her husband could save enough money to buy a house.

Early in 1928 Ruby and her three little girls boarded the steamship *Vulcania*, bound for Barbados. The trip from the U.S. mainland to the

West Indian island took nine days. After they landed, there was another long trip in a dusty bus to the small village where Mrs. Emily Seale lived. Mrs. Seale, a tall, erect woman was, says Shirley, "one of the few persons whose authority I would never dare to defy, or even question."

Ruby St. Hill stayed with her daughters for six months until she was sure they were accustomed to their grandmother and the tiny village. But when it came time for her to leave, the separation was painful for everyone. Shirley and her sisters cried and cried, and for several weeks they asked every day when she was coming back. After a while, though, they adjusted to their new lives in the big extended family that included, in addition to their grandmother, an aunt, an uncle, and four other grandchildren whose parents were also trying to make a life for themselves in the United States.

Shirley's grandmother was very strict, and Shirley learned to get along with others better and to share more. But she didn't lose her sense of independence or her "mouth." Sometimes even her older cousins would give in to her. There were many chores to be done on the farm, and Shirley did her share. She enjoyed the times when everyone gathered around the dinner table and talked, and Sundays when everyone dressed in their best and walked the two miles to church together.

When she was four, Shirley enrolled at the village school, which was actually the church. Seven classes were conducted in the same large room, separated only by blackboards. The school day was long, from eight to four, and the teachers were very strict. Any child who acted up was flogged with a rod, and Shirley came under the rod her share of times. But she looks back on the experience with gratitude. She learned to read and write by the time she was five.

The days passed into months and the months into years, and still Ruby St. Hill did not return for her daughters. In the United States, the Great Depression of the 1930s had caused prices to rise, so the St. Hills could not save as much as they had hoped. Also, Ruby St. Hill had given birth to a fourth daughter, Selma, and had had to stop working to take care of her. By the end of 1933 Charles and Ruby St. Hill realized they would have to put their dream of owning a house aside and bring their children home.

Shirley was nearly ten years old when her mother returned. She could not stop looking at her, or saying the words "my mother" over and over. Her joy at being reunited with her mother was tempered by the pain of leaving her grand-mother, whom she had come to love. She would always be grateful to her grandmother. "Granny gave me strength, dignity, and love," she says. "I didn't need the black revolution to teach me that."

Shirley had only the dimmest memories of Brooklyn, and the change was hard on her and her sisters, who did not remember the city at all. They could not get used to the sounds of cars and sirens. All the streets looked the same, and they were constantly getting lost.

School was the hardest adjustment for Shirley to make. At P.S. 84 she was put into the third grade, with students two years younger than she. In Barbados she would have been in the sixth form, which was equivalent to the sixth grade. The reason she was placed in the third grade was that in Barbados she had not been taught any American history or geography.

Shirley was angry and embarrassed to be in the third grade. She was also bored, because she already knew so much of the subject matter. She started throwing spitballs and flicking rubber bands at her classmates. She became a "behavior problem." Luckily, her teacher realized she was acting up because she was bored. On the teacher's advice, the school arranged for Shirley to have a private tutor, and in a year and a half she not only caught up to her grade level, but passed it.

Meanwhile, her education was continuing at home. Shirley's father always bought two or three newspapers a day and loved to talk about what was going on in the country and the world. Shirley adored him and hung on to his every word. He spoke often of politics, of the need for trade unions (he belonged to the Confectionary and Bakers International Union), and of prejudice by whites against blacks. Shirley listened and tried to understand, but she herself had never felt prejudice.

Their neighborhood was mostly Jewish, but

everyone got along. P.S. 84 was eighty percent white, and all Shirley's teachers were white, but she did not feel discriminated against. She knew she was a different color from her teachers and most of her fellow students, but she had been raised to feel pretty and bright and capable of success, as long as she worked hard for it.

Her feelings about racial differences changed when the family moved to a larger apartment in the Bedford-Stuyvesant section of Brooklyn. It was an area where about half the residents were black, mostly newly arrived from the South, and the older, Jewish residents felt threatened. For the first time Shirley heard racial slurs.

Shirley faced a similarly hostile atmosphere at her new school, P.S. 28, and after she skipped a grade, at J.H.S. 78. There were often racial incidents among the students, but Shirley kept out of them. She did not feel any discrimination from her teachers and continued to do well in school. The only discrimination she experienced was because she was a girl. She made higher grades than all the boys in her class, but she knew they considered her "just a girl." She was dimly aware of the fact that the great people in history they studied in school were mostly men.

In those days black history and women's history were not part of the curriculum. The only time blacks were mentioned was when slavery was discussed. The only woman they learned about was Betsy Ross. Shirley was lucky that her father was very knowledgeable about black history. He often mentioned the names of important black people of the past. Shirley went to the local library to find books about them, and soon became especially interested in the women. One of her heroines was Harriet Tubman, a slave who became the most famous "conductor" on the Underground Railroad.

Reading about Harriet Tubman led Shirley to an interest in Susan B. Anthony, a white woman who fought against slavery and whose house in Rochester, New York, served as a station for Harriet Tubman's Underground Railroad. Both Anthony and Tubman often spoke of how women in the United States at that time had much in common with blacks, because they could not vote and did not enjoy equal rights with men.

Shirley's parents had so much trouble paying rent on the new apartment that finally her mother had to take a job as a maid for a white family in the Flatbush section of Brooklyn. They could not afford a baby-sitter, so Shirley had to take on the responsibilities of caring for her younger sisters until her parents came home from work. She became a "latchkey child," carrying the apartment key on a string around her neck. She took her responsibilities very seriously, but her sisters accused her of being a bully and acting "like she was Mama."

Her experience as a latchkey child made Shirley understand the need for day care for the children of mothers who had to work. Later, she would fight for day-care programs.

Shirley graduated from Girls' High School in Brooklyn in 1942 and enrolled at Brooklyn College, where she majored in sociology. While still in college she began to go to local political meetings, but in those days a black person, especially a black woman, could not hope to run for political office. When she graduated from college, she looked for a job as a teacher and went to work at Mt. Calvary Child Care Center in Harlem. She also enrolled in night classes at Columbia University to earn a master's degree in education.

Shirley met her future husband, Conrad Chisholm, at Columbia. He was a detective with a private security company. She wasn't ready for marriage yet, but he was willing to wait. They were married in 1949, when Shirley was twenty-five, and moved into a house in Brooklyn.

Chisholm continued to go to political meetings, but she was fed up with the Democratic party and its unwillingness to treat blacks seriously. In 1953 she worked hard for a black candidate who ran for the post of civil judge as an independent. Her candidate won the election.

That same year, Chisholm was appointed director of a private nursery school in Brooklyn. Six years after that, she went to work for the New York City Division of Day Care. She and Conrad had wanted children, but after two miscarriages she decided to devote her life to other people's children.

By the early 1960s the nonviolent civil rights movement in the South was in full force. Chisholm admired Dr. Martin Luther King, Jr., but she was more interested in what Malcolm X had to say. A minister of the Nation of Islam, a black nationalist group, Malcolm X criticized black attempts at integration and stressed black self-help. Chisholm felt he understood black people who lived in cities. She and her father often discussed him and believed that any movement for dignity in the black community was healthy.

Chisholm joined a group of other blacks who were interested in politics to form the Unity Democratic Club in Brooklyn. Soon, it was the most powerful Democratic club in the area. In 1964 Chisholm decided to run for the state assembly. The men in the Unity Club made it clear that they felt a woman had no business running for political office, but Chisholm refused to back down. In November, after a long, hard campaign, she won the election.

Although she was not the first black New York State assemblywoman (Bessie Buchanan of Harlem had that distinction), Chisholm was determined to be the most active one. The first bill she introduced that became a law extended unemployment insurance coverage to domestic workers such as maids and cooks. As a member of the Committee on Education, she introduced bills to increase state aid to day-care centers and raise the amount of money spent on each public school pupil. Both these bills were passed. Elected to a second term in the assembly, Shirley Chisholm introduced the bill of which she was most proud. It created a program called SEEK that found deserving black and Hispanic high school students and gave them state scholarships to college.

In 1968 Chisholm decided to run for Congress from a newly created congressional district in her home area of Bedford-Stuyvesant in Brooklyn. Her campaign slogan was: "Fighting Shirley Chisholm — Unbought and Unbossed." She won the Democratic primary, and in Brooklyn that usually meant a sure victory in the November election. But this time the Republican candidate was James Farmer, a longtime activist who had worked hard in the civil rights movement and become nationally known.

Farmer directed his campaign toward the difference in their sexes: Shirley Chisholm was a nice little schoolteacher who meant well, but the new Twelfth Congressional District needed a *man*. Chisholm decided to answer Farmer's tactics by campaigning hard for the women's vote. In the November election she won more than two times the number of votes that Farmer received to become the first black woman in the U.S. House of Representatives.

Shirley Chisholm was also one of the few women and one of the few blacks in Congress, but she didn't let that bother her. She went right to work. She was named to the Agriculture Committee, but she refused to accept the assignment. She finally managed to get on the Veterans' Affairs Committee. It wasn't what she wanted, but as she said, "There are a lot more veterans in my district than there are trees."

As a new congresswoman, Chisholm knew she could not get any bills passed. So she concentrated on helping the people in her district obtain jobs or help with problems they were having with various government agencies. She spent long hours in her Brooklyn office. At her Washington, D.C., office, she found herself helping out poor people in the District of Columbia. These people had a representative in Congress, Walter Fauntroy, but since the District was not a state, he had no vote.

At the end of her first two-year term, Chisholm ran again for Congress and won. This time she got the committee assignment she wanted — Education and Labor. She decided not to try to introduce new laws, but to work with laws that were already in place but were not being used. In this way, she managed to get money for local Brooklyn organizations and to use laws against discrimination to help people find jobs, housing, day care, and welfare.

Around 1970 Shirley Chisholm was giving a speech at a college in the South. A white male student asked her why she didn't run for president. Chisholm answered, "You must understand, whatever my ability to handle the job, and regardless of your belief in me, I am black and I am a woman." But the student's question started her thinking, "Why not?"

The next presidential election was in 1972. The Republican president, Richard Nixon, would surely run again. Several Democrats, including Senators Hubert Humphrey of Minnesota, George McGovern of South Dakota, and Edmund Muskie of Maine, planned to seek their party's nomination. Chisholm knew it was a gamble for a black woman to enter the contest against them.

But conditions for women in the United States were beginning to change. The 1970s women's movement had started. Taking their cues from the nonviolent civil rights movement, women began to demand equal rights and to demonstrate for those rights. For the first time many women, not just a few, were asking, "Why not a woman president?"

College students and women's groups urged Chisholm to run. Black women urged her to run. Almost every politician, black or white, urged her not to. So Shirley Chisholm decided to try.

On January 25, 1972, she announced her candidacy: "I stand before you today as a candidate for the Democratic nomination for the presidency of the United States. I am not the candidate of black America, although I am black and proud. I am not the candidate for the women's movement of this country, although I am a woman, and I am equally proud of that. I am not the candidate of any political bosses or special interests. . . . I am the candidate of the people."

Shirley Chisholm was the first black woman ever to run for the presidential nomination of a major party. She was only the second woman ever to run. In 1964 Senator Margaret Chase Smith of Maine had entered two primaries for the Republican presidential nomination. Chisholm decided to use her campaign to speak out on behalf of neglected Americans — minorities and women and also children. She was strongly against the Vietnam War. She was a strong supporter of abortion rights and the rights of homosexuals, of welfare and tax reform.

The candidate of a major political party must win a number of primary elections, which choose delegates to the party's national convention. Chisholm started her campaign in Florida, where a primary was to be held in February. She did not have much money, and her campaign organization in that state was really a series of existing organizations that had volunteered to help her.

Soon the women's groups were complaining that the blacks were trying to take over. Blacks complained that women were trying to take over. Women portrayed Chisholm as a woman's candidate; blacks campaigned for her as a black candidate. Chisholm tried to make peace among these groups, but she was also busy making appearances to raise money. Then, too, she was still a congresswoman and had to be in Washington, D.C., much of the time. She won only four percent of the vote in the Florida primary.

But she pressed on. In March, April, and May, she campaigned in New Jersey, Massachusetts,

California, Michigan, and North Carolina. In each state, her volunteers fought over who she was supposed to represent. Chisholm tried to smooth things out, but she found that the women were especially hard to deal with. "Even more than the blacks, I think, they showed the effects of their past exclusion from the political process," she said later, "and unlike blacks, they found it hard to believe that they had a great deal to learn."

Although Shirley Chisholm had strong opinions on many issues and was not afraid to express them, some people criticized her for not having a clear platform, or list of things she would do if elected. They complained that her platform was herself. She answered her critics by saying that she was forced to campaign on the issue of herself because everywhere she went people questioned her qualifications to be president. They didn't ask the same of her opponents.

"The others could point to years of experience in the Senate or in the House or as a governor of some state," she explained. "What could I point to but years of working my way up through grassroots politics, fighting past barriers every step of the way, partly because I was black but mostly because I was a woman. I made it within the system in spite of the system, and that was one of the major thrusts of my campaign. It was all those men who'd had years of experience in law and in Congress and as governors who'd gotten us into the mess we're in in the first place."

Chisholm did her best to shake up the system,

and as primary after primary took place, she received enough votes to keep her going. While the percentages were small, they showed that her message was getting through to some people. When she won five percent of the vote in the California primary, she became entitled to Secret Service protection. She didn't really think she needed it, but it made her feel like a real candidate. She had never expected to win. Her reason for running was to give the neglected groups in American society a real choice.

With the Democratic national convention a month away, Chisholm had just a small number of delegates, but she planned to stay in the campaign. She hoped that by convention time, the black male politicians who had fought her or ignored her during the campaign would support her. But when the convention got under way in Miami in July, she found that the black men had decided to throw their weight behind Senator George McGovern.

At the convention she pleaded with black delegates to at least support her on the first ballot, and not just give their votes to McGovern. She urged them to make him give them some promises in return for their votes.

Shirley Chisholm was officially nominated on Wednesday night, July 12, by Percy Sutton, black president of the Borough of Manhattan in New York City. Her nomination was seconded by Charles Evers, the black mayor of Fayette, Mississippi. He also urged black delegates to vote for her on the first ballot, "so the black poor and other people who have been left out for so long will not be in someone's pocket on the first ballot."

But George McGovern won on the first ballot, and Shirley Chisholm's long campaign was over. She supported the choice of her party, but she did not intend to do much work for him. In the general election in November, George McGovern lost to the incumbent Republican president, Richard Nixon.

Chisholm believed that she had made a difference. She had been the reason why many blacks had registered to vote for the first time. She had inspired many women to become involved in politics for the first time. She had blazed the trail. If she had not run for president, perhaps Geraldine Ferraro, the congresswoman from Queens, would not have run for vice president of the United States in 1984. Perhaps Jesse Jackson would not have run for president in 1984 and 1988.

Chisholm returned to her work as a congresswoman and fought for the same issues she had talked about as a candidate. She worked to save the Office of Economic Opportunity, which had distributed funds to antipoverty programs for several years but which the Nixon Administration wanted to disband. She worked on behalf of an Equal Rights Amendment to the Constitution that would ensure equal rights for women. She worked especially hard for a Minimum Wage Bill, and was delighted when it passed both houses of Congress. But she was terribly disappointed when President Nixon vetoed it.

Angry and discouraged, Shirley announced in July 1973 that she intended to retire from politics. She was tired of fighting for bills that were not passed into law. She knew that a congressperson had to serve for many years before gaining the seniority and power necessary to have laws passed. She didn't feel like waiting. But she was not a quitter. She remained in Congress several more years and in 1976 became the first black and first woman to serve in the House leadership as secretary to the Democratic caucus.

Shirley and Conrad Chisholm had grown apart over the years, in some measure because Shirley was so busy and so often away from home. They were divorced in February 1977. The following September, Shirley married Arthur Hardwick, Jr., an architectural designer whom she had met thirteen years earlier when both were in the New York State Assembly.

In 1980 Arthur Hardwick was seriously injured in an automobile accident. He spent ten months in the hospital, and recuperated at home for many more months. Chisholm decided that she wanted to spend more time at home with her husband. Shirley Chisholm left Congress in 1982, after serving seven full terms and after twenty-five years in politics.

She accepted a position at Mount Holyoke College, teaching courses on politics, race, and women. She became chairwoman of the National Political Caucus of Black Women. She continues to speak out on political issues and advises other women to enter politics, saying, "I don't believe there are really going to be real changes in America until women are in decision- and policy-making positions in this nation."

11
Malcolm X

M alcolm X was born Malcolm Little. He took an *X* for his last name when he was in his twenties. The *X* stood for his long-lost African name, and it replaced the name that had been given to his family by some white master back in the time of slavery.

At the time he took the *X* for his last name, Malcolm hated white people for what they had done to blacks. He believed that blacks should not try to become integrated into white society. Instead, he believed that blacks should create their own society. He was a black nationalist and a black separatist. The experiences he'd had in his life had made him bitter against white America.

Malcolm X was born in Omaha, Nebraska, on May 19, 1925. He received his first lessons in black nationalism from his father, the Reverend Earl

Little. The older man was a follower of Marcus Garvey, a black leader who urged his people to form their own businesses and organizations and not depend on whites. Garvey also had the idea that blacks should go to Africa, the home of their ancestors, and establish their own nations.

The family moved around a lot, partly because word would travel around the white community that the Reverend Little was trying to stir up trouble. But wherever he went the Reverend Little tried to convince other blacks to join Garvey's organization, the United Negro Improvement Organization. When the family moved to Lansing, Michigan, he held secret meetings and talked about becoming independent of whites. A local white group called the Black Legion decided to put a stop to his activities. In 1929, when Malcolm was four, two white men set fire to their home. In 1931, when Malcolm was six, his father was murdered.

Malcolm's mother was left with eight children and no way to provide for her family. She went on welfare, but the money she received still was not enough. When Malcolm was ten his mother could no longer stand the stress of trying to keep her family together. She suffered a mental breakdown and was placed in a state mental hospital. The family was broken up, and the children were sent to foster homes.

Malcolm lived with foster families until he was expelled from school for putting a tack on his teacher's chair. He was sent to a detention home

that was run by a white couple named Swerling. The Swerlings understood that he was a troubled boy and were kind to him. Instead of going on to reform school, like most of the other boys at the detention home, Malcolm stayed with the Swerlings.

He was the first boy from the home to attend the local junior high school. He was also one of the few blacks. But he did well and was elected president of his seventh-grade class.

Then Ella, the Reverend Little's daughter by a former marriage, came from Boston to visit Malcolm. She invited him to spend the summer with her in Boston. There, for the first time in his life, Malcolm was in a place where there were a lot of black people. Back in Michigan for the start of school, he felt uncomfortable around so many whites. He wanted to go back to Boston, and Ella arranged for him to be put in her custody. Ella wanted Malcolm to go to school and make friends in the respectable area of Boston where she lived. However, he soon started hanging around with a crowd of teenagers who gambled and used drugs. Their kind of life seemed much more exciting to him. Instead of going to school, Malcolm got a job shining shoes at the Roseland State Ballroom. When he was seventeen he lied about his age and got a job as a railroad porter.

This job gave him a chance to go to New York, and he fell in love with Harlem the first time he saw it. After he was fired from his railroad job, he moved to Harlem. There, he also made friends with a crowd who gambled and drank and used drugs. When asked where he was from, he would just say "Detroit," which was the largest city in Michigan. Because his hair was a reddish color, his new friends soon gave him the nickname "Detroit Red."

Malcolm became a hustler, picking up money by peddling dope, doing small burglary jobs, and running a gambling game called "the numbers." Eventually he got into trouble with another numbers runner. Fearing for his life, he went back to Boston.

In Boston he turned to the same kinds of hustles before joining a burglary ring with four others. For a while the ring was successful, but eventually they were caught. In February 1946, when Malcolm was not yet twenty-one, he was convicted of burglary and sentenced to ten years in prison.

Malcolm was bitter over what had happened to him. He was so unruly in prison that he spent most of his time in solitary confinement. Fellow prisoners gave him the nickname "Satan." He had been in prison about two years when he received a letter from his older brother, Philbert, who was living in Detroit. In the letter, his brother told him that he had discovered the true religion for the black man, the Nation of Islam. Malcolm learned that most of his brothers and sisters were in Detroit and followers of Elijah Muhammad, leader of the Nation of Islam.

Founded in the early 1930s by W. D. Fard, the

Nation of Islam was supposed to be a part of the
world religion of Islam. Islam is the religion of
the Arab world and parts of Africa, Malaysia, and
elsewhere. It includes members of all races and
does not usually teach racial hatred, but W. D.
Fard's version did. So did that of Fard's successor
as leader of the Nation, Elijah Muhammad. Based
in Chicago, Elijah Muhammad had strenghtened
and enlarged the Nation, although it was still
very small. In 1950 membership was about 3,000.

Like followers of the world religion of Islam,
members of the Nation of Islam believed that
there was only one God, Allah. They also believed
that Allah had come to America and made Himself known to Elijah Muhammad. Allah had told
Elijah that the devil, who was doomed, was the
white man. Because slavery had ripped the black
people in Africa from their homeland, they did
not know who their ancestors were or even their
ancestral names. They were a lost people. But
now Allah had come to Elijah Muhammad to proclaim that they had been found. They were the
Lost-Found Nation of Islam, and they and other
dark peoples would rule the world again.

As in the world religion of Islam, there were
dietary rules in the Nation of Islam. Believers,
who were known as Muslims, were not to eat
pork, because the pig was considered a dirty animal. They were not to smoke cigarettes, drink
liquor, or take drugs, because their bodies were
temples to Allah, and these things were not good
for the body.

Malcolm thought about the teachings of Elijah Muhammad and decided they made sense. In the letters he kept receiving from his brothers and sisters he learned that they were all doing well and feeling a great pride and dignity. He wanted to feel that way, too. He sat down and wrote a letter to Elijah Muhammad, but was ashamed of what he produced. His schooling had stopped at junior high. His handwriting was terrible, and he could not find the words to express what he felt.

In order to improve his vocabulary, he got a dictionary. In order to improve his handwriting, he began to copy the dictionary. Eventually Malcolm copied the entire dictionary! Day after day, and night after night, he educated himself. Now that he had a better vocabulary, he could read books, and he spent as much time as he could at the prison library. He wanted to find proof of Mr. Muhammad's teachings, and in the course of his search he discovered the history of his own race.

Malcolm spent as much time as he could reading in his cell. When the lights were turned out at ten P.M., he moved from his bunk to the floor of his cell, so he could read by the light of the red emergency bulb in the hallway outside. He read about the great civilizations that had existed in Africa before the arrival of European colonists. He read about the horrors of slavery. He learned about the many contributions that blacks had made to America. He began to feel a great pride in being black, and he felt that he owed his new-found pride to Mr. Muhammad. He began to write to Mr. Muhammad every single day, and to his surprise, Mr. Muhammad began to write back to him.

Mr. Muhammad urged Malcolm to pray to Allah, and that was very hard for Malcolm to do. Since the death of his father, Malcolm had relied only on himself. It was hard to accept the idea of asking a higher power for help. In later years he joked that the only time he'd gotten down on his knees was to pick a lock. But finally he got down on his knees and prayed to Allah, and he began to feel a sense of inner peace he had never known before.

Malcolm began talking to his fellow black prisoners about what he was learning, and about the Nation of Islam. He joined the weekly debates that were held at the prison. The debates were on all sorts of subjects, from the pros and cons of compulsory military training to the real identity of the great English playwright William Shakespeare. Malcolm read about all these subjects and became an expert debater. But so much reading by poor light after "lights out" caused his eyes to weaken, and he had to start wearing glasses.

In the spring of 1952 the Massachusetts State Parole Board voted that Malcolm should be released. He walked out of the prison gate in August. He immediately boarded a bus to Detroit, where he had been invited to stay with his brother Wilfred and his family.

He began to go to services at Muslim Temple Number One in Detroit. He was impressed by the families of neatly dressed members, by the air of dignity they had. He liked the idea that members of the temple had started their own grocery stores and restaurants and schools. But he was troubled that there were empty seats at the services and wondered why the Muslims did not try to recruit more members instead of waiting for new members to come to them. He applied for membership in the Nation of Islam. In the official letter of approval from Muslim headquarters in Chicago, he received his *X*, his Muslim last name.

On the Sunday before Labor Day, the members of the Detroit temple traveled in a caravan of cars to Chicago to attend services at Temple Number Two. Malcolm was overjoyed to meet Elijah Muhammad, whom he looked up to as a father. He wanted to help Mr. Muhammad and suggested that the Muslims do more recruiting. Muhammad told him to go ahead and try, and soon Malcolm was out in the streets doing what the Muslims came to call "fishing."

All the reading he had done in prison and the skills he had built debating in prison came in very handy now. He gave speeches wherever he could, and was soon attracting new members to Temple Number One. The following year, Mr. Muhammad named him assistant minister of the temple.

Then Mr. Muhammad began to train Malcolm to spread the word of the Nation of Islam to other cities. Malcolm established Muslim temples in Boston and Philadelphia. Mr. Muhammad rewarded him by naming him minister of Temple Number Seven in New York City.

Malcolm met Sister Betty X at Temple Number Seven. They fell in love, married, and moved into a house in Queens, New York, which the Nation of Islam bought for them. Their first daughter, Attilah, was born in 1958.

By 1959 membership in the Nation of Islam was over 100,000 — large enough to attract the attention of the white media, who were concerned about the Muslims preaching hatred of whites. That year a television program was devoted to the Muslims. Called "The Hate That Hate Produced," it stressed the Nation's anti-white preachings and caused a sensation. Not only white leaders, but also moderate black leaders such as Dr. Martin Luther King, Jr., denounced the Muslims as "black segregationists" and "black supremacists."

As minister of the Muslim temple in New York, the media center of the world, Malcolm was besieged by reporters who asked him to respond to these charges. He was pleased to do so:

> The white man so guilty of white supremacy can't hide his guilt by trying to accuse The Honorable Elijah Muhammad of teaching black supremacy and hate! . . .
>
> For the white man to ask the black man if he hates him is just like . . . the

wolf asking the sheep, *"Do you hate me?" The white man is in no moral position to accuse anyone else of hate.*

Malcolm X was such an intelligent man and such a fine public speaker that reporters returned to him again and again to get his views on all sorts of subjects, including political issues. It was clear that they regarded him as the chief spokesman for the Nation of Islam.

Malcolm X saw these interviews as a way to spread the word about the Nation of Islam, but he went further than just talking about the religion. Although Mr. Muhammad did not want any of his spokesmen to make statements about political and social subjects, Malcolm could not resist doing so. He believed that the Nation had a duty to voice opinions about what was going on in the United States.

For example, Malcolm spoke out against the nonviolent civil rights struggle being led by Dr. Martin Luther King, Jr., and other moderate black ministers in the South. He couldn't understand why people would choose not to fight back against the violence that was being done to them by whites. Elijah Muhammad did not want him taking a stand on this issue.

Malcolm X was always careful to refer to Mr. Muhammad as the leader of the Nation, and he believed that Mr. Muhammad trusted him as a loyal follower. He began to hear of grumblings in the Nation of Islam that he was overshadowing

Mr. Muhammad. But he thought this was just jealousy. In fact, Mr. Muhammad had once told him that he would be envied. In 1963 Mr. Muhammad seemed to show he still trusted Malcolm X by naming him the Nation's first national minister. But in private Elijah Muhammad was saying that Malcolm X was dangerous because of his outspokenness and would someday turn against Elijah Muhammad.

When Malcolm learned about Muhammad's private opinion, he was deeply shaken. He felt as if his father had turned against him. He started to refuse interviews and invitations to speak, hoping to divert some of the attention away from himself. Then he learned that Elijah Muhammad had been guilty for years of breaking the strictest moral law of the Nation of Islam: the law against adultery. He was deeply disappointed in the man he had looked up to for so long. He was also afraid of what would happen to the Nation of Islam if the public ever found out.

Worried and under great pressure, Malcolm made a public statement that he would later regret. In November 1963 President John F. Kennedy was assassinated in Dallas, Texas. Malcolm believed that the president had been killed because there was so much hatred in America. He said it was a case of "chickens coming home to roost." But the public took the statement to mean that somehow the president deserved to be killed. There was a huge outcry. Elijah Muhammad told Malcolm that his statement was rash, poorly timed, and bad for the Muslims. He silenced Malcolm for ninety days.

Malcolm thought that meant that he could make no public statements for three months. But he soon learned that he could not even teach in his own temple. Then a trusted assistant confessed that he had been ordered to kill him. Malcolm realized that his life in the Nation of Islam was over.

By this time he and Betty had two more daughters, Qubilah, born in 1960, and Ilyasah, born in 1962. Malcolm did not know what he was going to do to support them. He did know that he must continue speaking out for the cause of black people. He decided to form a new organization that would include black people of all religions. He called it Muslim Mosque, Inc. Unlike the Nation of Islam, his organization would actively work for political and economic power for black people. But he wasn't sure how to proceed.

His basic beliefs had been badly shaken. He could no longer believe in Elijah Muhammad or in the Nation of Islam as preached by Elijah Muhammad. He had read enough to know that the world religion of Islam was different, and he still believed in Allah. He decided to make a pilgrimage to Mecca, the most holy shrine of Islam, in Saudi Arabia. His half sister Ella in Boston agreed to help him finance the trip.

Every Muslim is supposed to make a pilgrimage to Mecca at least once in his lifetime. Malcolm X was only one of thousands and thousands of

Muslims who made the pilgrimage, and he was amazed to see that Muslims were people of all races. They traveled and ate and slept together without regard to race or nationality. Malcolm was struck by the strong sense of brotherhood among these people. He realized that the world religion of Islam was not anti-white at all.

He wrote back home,

> *America needs to understand Islam, because this is the one religion that erases from its society the race problem. Throughout my travels in the Muslim world, I have met, talked to, and eaten with people who in America would have been considered "white" — but the "white" attitude was removed from their minds because of the religion of Islam. I have never before seen sincere and true brotherhood practiced by all colors together irrespective of their color.*

While he was abroad, Malcolm also visited several African countries and met with their leaders. These countries were newly independent from their European colonial rulers, and Malcolm could see that they shared some of the same problems with blacks in the United States. Both Africans and African Americans were trying to become economically independent of whites. He believed that the two peoples could help and learn from each other.

When he returned to the United States, Malcolm X knew what he wanted to do. He formed a new group, the Organization of Afro-American Unity (OAAU). Like Muslim Mosque, Inc., it would work for black political and economic power. He called it a black nationalist organization.

In 1964, the year his fourth daughter, Amilah, was born, Malcolm X made a second pilgrimage to Mecca and spent much more time with African leaders on this second trip. He also met with the white American ambassador to one of the African countries and was astonished at something the ambassador told him.

The ambassador said that when he was in Africa he never thought in terms of race, but that when he returned to America he again became aware of racial differences. Malcolm said to him, "What you are telling me is that it isn't the American white *man* who is racist, but it's the American political, economic, and social *atmosphere* that automatically nourishes a racist psychology in the white man." The ambassador agreed.

When he returned again to the United States, Malcolm stopped calling the OAAU a black nationalist organization. He now stressed that whites were welcome to be part of the organization, as long as they were committed to equal power for blacks.

Meanwhile, the Nation of Islam had gone to court to evict Malcolm's family from the house in Queens where they were living. He received many threatening telephone calls. At least three times he and his followers were confronted by armed Muslims. On February 13, 1965, the house was hit by gasoline bombs.

Although no one was hurt, Malcolm realized he had to get his family out of that house. Betty was pregnant again, and he was afraid for his family's safety. They went house-hunting and found a house in another part of Queens that they wanted to buy.

Malcolm hoped that telling the public about the threats on his life might make those who wished to kill him think twice about acting.

Malcolm believed he was now a greater threat to white racists than he had been when he was a Black Muslim. After all, as a Black Muslim he was part of a small, radical group that many blacks and whites did not take seriously. As long as he was preaching black nationalism, he could not have a broad appeal. But once he started talking about working together with whites to change the American political and economic system, whites who were against integration became worried that he would become too powerful.

On Sunday, February 21, 1965, Malcolm X walked onto the stage of the Audubon Ballroom on West 166th Street in Harlem. The occasion was a meeting of the OAAU. The ballroom was crowded with members and curious onlookers. Malcolm greeted his audience and was just about to begin speaking when a scuffle broke out in the rear of the hall. Everyone turned to look, and at that moment two men ran down the center aisle toward the stage, firing at Malcolm X, and killing him.

Three Black Muslim men were later convicted of assassinating Malcolm X and sentenced to life imprisonment. At this writing, they are still in jail.

After Malcolm X's death, his organization, the OAAU, disbanded.

The Nation of Islam continued to grow. By 1975 membership was 300,000, which proved to be its peak. That same year Elijah Muhammad died and the Nation split into two factions. Both continue to exist today, but with much smaller memberships.

Malcolm X was killed three months before his fortieth birthday. He did not live to see his twin daughters born, nor to watch any of his six daughters grow up.

He also did not live to pursue his dream of a strong organization that would work with whites to see that blacks gained economic and political independence. But that dream remained alive, as did his memory.

Twenty-five years after his death, many people believe that, had he lived, he would have become an even more powerful black leader than he had been as Minister Malcolm X.

He might never have been as loved and respected as Martin Luther King, Jr. But he might have been the kind of leader black Americans needed. After Dr. King was himself assassinated in 1968, there were no black leaders of the stature of Dr. King and Malcolm X. Malcolm X might have offered new directions.

His memory lives on as an example of what one man can do in spite of many barriers. And the fame and respect his name commands even now show that killers may murder a man but not the ideas for which he stands.

12
Ronald McNair

Dr. Ronald McNair died when the space shuttle *Challenger* blew up in January 1986. He and his six fellow astronauts, including the first civilian astronaut, teacher Christa McAuliffe, will always be remembered as heroes who helped to conquer space. While perhaps no victory is worth the loss of young and vital people, it is fitting that the astronauts who died in the *Challenger* were such a mixed group. There were two women, one Asian American, and one African American, in addition to three white men. All were serving a country that prides itself on giving equal opportunity to everyone, regardless of race or sex. Ronald McNair, Ellison Onizuka, Judith Resnick, and Christa McAuliffe all chose to take advantage of that opportunity. Ronald McNair, being black, had to work the hardest.

Ronald Erwin McNair was born October 21,

1950, in Lake City, South Carolina. His mother, Pearl, was a schoolteacher in the black schools, which were separate from and not equal to the white schools. His father, Carl, was an automobile mechanic who had not completed high school. Carl McNair deeply regretted not having finished school, and he insisted that his three sons get the education he had not received.

Ronald was the second of three boys. His older brother was named Carl, Jr., the younger, Eric. They lived in a big, old, weatherbeaten, unpainted wooden house on Moore Street in Lake City. It belonged to Carl McNair's family. Ronald's grandfather had been a bishop in the Church of God movement, and there was a church in the yard. By the time Ronald was born, Bishop McNair had died, but the church was still active.

Ron and his family shared the house with his grandmother, great-grandmother, and assorted aunts and uncles and cousins. Everyone worked hard to help out the family, and even the little children had chores to do as soon as they were able.

Ron's great-grandmother took care of the young children before they entered school. She began teaching them to read right away. She herself could not write, so they had to wait until they started school to learn that. By the time he was three years old, Ron was reading some words, and by the time he was four his family felt he was ready for school.

The Lake City schools would not take such a

young child, so the family took him to the principal of Camerontown Elementary School in the nearby countryside. He attended school at Camerontown with older, rural children until he was five and eligible to enroll at the black school nearest his home in Lake City.

There, his teacher Mrs. Jones was struck by how serious he was. He always had a pencil behind his ear and a notebook in his hand. She saw him as a bright loner who would go out to the playground with his class, lie on the ground, stare up into the sky, and smile. He did well in school, and in fact was always ahead of his classmates in the work the class was doing. But he did not become bored. He could always read ahead in the textbook. Science was his favorite subject.

He carried a slide rule around in his back pocket. His classmates nicknamed him "Gismo," which is a slang term for a machine part. When the Soviet Union launched the first space vehicle, *Sputnik*, in 1957, seven-year-old Ron was so excited that, according to an elementary-school classmate, he walked around saying "Sputnik, Sputnik, Sputnik" all the time.

Music was a close second to science as Ron's favorite subject. In the beginning of his seventh-grade year, he started taking band, and it was typical of the way he applied himself that by Christmas he was playing saxophone in the marching band.

Learning did not stop when school was over. At home, Ron and his brothers were expected to

read. His parents bought them the *World Book Encyclopedia,* and the boys spent Saturday mornings reading from *A* through *Z.*

In the summers, and during school vacations, Ron and his brothers worked in the nearby cotton fields. It was hard, backbreaking work, but they did not complain. Later on, Ron said, "I gained qualities in that cotton field. I got tough. I learned to endure. I refused to quit."

In many ways, Lake City was still the Old South, where most blacks worked in the cotton and tobacco fields and lived in poverty. Schools, libraries, drinking fountains, and buses were segregated. Few blacks were allowed to register to vote. The civil rights movement of the 1950s took a long time to come to Lake City, and the Ku Klux Klan was active there well into the 1960s. When Ron was a boy, Klan members would ride around at night and fire their guns into the homes of blacks who were working for equal rights, especially the right to vote. Ron's family was never attacked, but they were fearful of the Klan.

When the children asked why the Klan hated black people, and why there was segregation, the elder McNairs could only assure them that they were as good as anyone else and could be anything they wanted. But it was difficult living under those conditions. When Ron was ten his father left the family to live in the North. Carl McNair moved to East Harlem in New York City, but he returned to Lake City every summer and sometimes at holidays. He participated with his wife in major decisions affecting the family and was available when his sons needed him.

In the summers Carl McNair coached local boys' baseball teams. Ron was always on them. He was not only good at his schoolwork, he was also an excellent athlete. In fact, he excelled at whatever he tried. At Carver High School, named after the black scientist George Washington Carver, he was on the basketball, baseball, and football teams and also played saxophone in the school band. He won awards in physics and a science fair award for a rocket project. When he graduated he was valedictorian of the senior class.

There was no question that he would go to college, as his older brother, Carl, Jr., had before him. One of his aunts helped him to get a scholarship to North Carolina Agricultural and Technical College in Greensboro, where Carl, Jr., was enrolled. Established in 1891 as the Agricultural and Mechanical College for the Colored Race, the school had educated generations of black students who were barred from white colleges. North Carolina A&T also had a proud recent tradition. In 1960 some of its black students had staged sit-ins at the local Woolworth's lunch counter and sparked a student sit-in movement against segregation across the South. By the time Ronald McNair entered North Carolina A&T, white colleges were no longer segregated. But many black students felt more comfortable attending a black college.

McNair wasn't sure if he was good enough to major in physics, which is what he secretly wanted to do. He finally sought the help of a guidance counselor at the school, who gave him a group of tests. Based on the results of those tests, the counselor recommended that McNair major in science. "You're good enough," she said, and Ron took her advice.

He kept his interest in music and played his saxophone in a student rhythm-and-blues band that played at campus clubs and dances at local high schools. He also took up karate in his spare time and came to love the discipline and grace of it. He took classes at the local YMCA until he won his black belt, then he started his own karate club at the college.

North Carolina A&T had just reorganized its physics department when McNair chose to major in science, and he became one of the department's star pupils. He spent part of one semester in an exchange program at Massachusetts Institute of Technology (MIT) in Cambridge, one of the best science schools in the nation. Coming from an all-black school to one that was mostly white was a big change for him, but his family had instilled in him a great pride in himself and he did not feel awkward. He recognized that MIT had the kinds of courses he wanted to take, and he determined to go there after he graduated from North Carolina A&T.

By taking a heavy course load, McNair managed to graduate early. In fact, he and his older brother, Carl, were in the same graduating class. It was a proud moment for the McNair family, for the two brothers were the first men in the family to graduate from college. There were other proud McNair graduates that June. Ron's and Carl's younger brother, Eric, graduated from high school. So did their grandmother, Mabel Montgomery, who received her high school diploma at the age of sixty-five.

The following September Ron entered the doctoral program in physics at MIT. His tuition and fees were paid by a Ford Foundation scholarship for black graduate students. At MIT he soon realized that he was not as well prepared academically as many of his fellow students, even though he had graduated with high honors from North Carolina A&T. But he determined to catch up by working extra hard. He was fortunate to have Michael Feld as his adviser. The two became close friends. McNair taught Feld karate. Feld taught McNair physics. He encouraged McNair to do extra study in the field.

McNair's special field of study was laser physics. Laser stands for *l*ight *a*mplification by *s*imulated *e*mission of *r*adiation. It uses atoms to generate electromagnetic waves in the visible part of the spectrum. To earn his doctorate, McNair had to write a dissertation and he spent nearly two years doing experiments and collecting data for it. Then a flood destroyed all his notes. But he spent only a short time worrying about the loss. Soon, he was back in the laboratory redoing the experiments. In three or four months, he had compiled all the data again.

"That's what kind of student he was," said Feld. "He was able to bring all of his skills — perseverence, resourcefulness, intelligence, good hands in the lab and the ability to work intensively —to bear on a scientific problem to get the job done."

While he was at work on his dissertation, Ron met Cheryl Moore at services at St. Paul's Church. Cheryl was a teacher in Cherry Hill, New Jersey, and the two were immediately attracted to one another. They married soon afterward in the same church where they had met.

McNair earned his doctorate from MIT in 1976. Around that same time, he received a flier about the space shuttle program. Becoming an astronaut seemed the perfect next step in his career. He had always been interested in space, from the time as a first-grader when he would lie on the playground and look up into the sky and smile. In high school McNair had won a prize in a science fair for a rocket project. His specialty, laser physics, was a field that had many applications to the astronaut and shuttle programs. He was aware that there were no blacks in the astronaut program, but as he said some years later, "I figured if they were sincere about the qualifications, I had a good chance at it." He applied to the program.

The U.S. space program had begun in 1958 after the 1957 launch of the Soviet Union's *Sput-*

nik I. Sputnik I, an unmanned space capsule, managed to achieve orbit and orbited earth for 184 days. Americans did not want Russians to conquer space first, and when he was elected in 1960 President John F. Kennedy made the space program a major goal. The following year, Commander Alan Shepard became the first American in space when he took a fifteen-minute ride on *Freedom 7*, America's first space vehicle. *Freedom 7* went up into the air and then came right back down again, but it was a start.

At first all the astronauts in the NASA program were white, and there was discrimination in the program. President Kennedy appointed the first black astronaut to the program in 1962. Captain Edward Dwight, a pilot in the Air Force, was in the program four years. The Air Force claimed that he failed to complete his training, but Dwight later said that he quit under pressure: "They didn't want black involvement. They felt that to send blacks into space would lessen the general public's enthusiasm for the space program."

After President Kennedy was assassinated, Vice President Lyndon Johnson became president. He appointed the second black astronaut, Bob Lawrence. But Lawrence died in a plane crash soon afterward. No other blacks were in the NASA program for about ten years.

By the middle 1970s NASA was under pressure to include blacks in its programs, and the agency responded to that pressure by starting a drive to recruit minorities. They hired Nichelle Nicholas, who had starred as Uhura in the popular TV series *Star Trek*, to do advertisements and give speeches at black schools and to community groups. They sent fliers to the science departments of black colleges as well as white colleges like MIT. They made efforts to ensure that black candidates had equal opportunity to apply to the program as white candidates. But whoever was chosen had to pass the same scrutiny.

While he was waiting to hear from the National Aeronautics and Space Administration (NASA), Ron and Cheryl McNair moved to Los Angeles, California, where he had accepted a job as a staff physicist at the Hughes Research Laboratories. He worked there until January 1978, when he learned he had been selected as an astronaut.

When Ronald McNair entered the NASA program, two other blacks were also admitted to the seventy-eight-member group of astronauts. The others were Guion Bluford and Fred Gregory. There were also women, including Sally Ride, who would later become the first American woman in space.

The McNairs moved to Houston to be near the headquarters of the Johnson Space Center. While there were many churches in the area, they chose to attend Antioch Baptist Church, a ninety-minute drive away. Not only did McNair attend that church on Sunday, he also drove there two other times every week to teach karate to local youngsters. The McNairs' first child, Reginald Ervin, was born in Houston and baptized at Antioch Baptist Church.

By the time Ronald McNair entered the NASA program, America's interests in space had changed. In the beginning the push was toward manned space flights and exploration *and* on surpassing the Soviet Union's accomplishments. On July 20, 1969, Neil Armstrong and Edwin Aldrin made America proud by becoming the first human beings to land on the moon.

In the early 1970s the United States continued manned exploration with *Skylab,* an earth-orbiting space station. *Skylab* was first launched by an unmanned booster rocket; the crews arrived later in another craft that docked to the main capsule.

After 1972, however, technology had been developed that allowed unmanned craft to explore space. The Mariner and Viking programs studied Venus and Mars. The Pioneer Program studied the outer planets and more distant space. Each program resulted in more knowledge of the solar system and beyond.

But by the mid-1970s Americans were no longer as interested in space exploration for its own sake. Sending rockets into space, whether manned or unmanned, cost a lot of money. The national feeling was that the space program ought to start paying for itself by building reusable spacecraft that could have a commercial purpose. The space shuttle program was developed to meet this demand.

NASA started to build the space shuttle in 1972. It is part rocket because it is propelled by rockets. It is part spacecraft because it can navigate in outer space. And it is part airplane because it has delta wings and can glide on air currents. The shuttle is capable of carrying "payloads," such as weather and communications satellites that government and private corporations are willing to pay to have launched. The shuttle can do work in space, such as build space stations. Shuttle astronauts can also perform tasks in space such as conducting scientific experiments requested by government and private corporations.

When McNair joined the astronaut program, NASA was getting ready to launch the first space shuttle and wanted to train shuttle astronauts.

All the new astronaut candidates went through the same basic training. For six months they attended classes in geology, medicine, aerodynamics, communications, astronomy, and shuttle systems. Then they visited all the different NASA space centers — Kennedy at Cape Canaveral, Florida; Marshall Space Flight Center in Huntsville, Alabama, where shuttle engines were developed; and Rockwell Aircraft Company in California, where the shuttles were built. Finally, in Houston at the Johnson Space Flight Center, they spent three months working on different aspects of the shuttle program, such as the mechanical arm that is used to move payloads in and out of the spacecraft's cargo bay and on different experiments in the space lab program.

After a year of training, the astronaut candidates became full-fledged astronauts. The first shuttle launching was still two years away, so all went to work in the shuttle program while they continued to train for the time when they would actually fly in the shuttle.

Some trained as shuttle pilots, others as mission specialists. The pilots flew the shuttle. The mission specialists were experts in the various types of cargo the shuttles would carry and trained to conduct experiments, operate the mechanical arm, launch satellites, and do all the other things the shuttle was up in space to do. Ronald McNair trained as a mission specialist.

All of the astronauts spent time both in Houston at the Johnson Space Flight Center and in California at the Rockwell Aircraft Company flying in shuttle simulators, which were machines that imitated the look and feel of the shuttle. In these shuttle simulators, they learned how it would feel to be flying in the shuttle and how to navigate it. But they all looked forward to the day when they would be able to fly in the real thing.

Columbia, the first space shuttle, was launched in April 1981. It completed its fourth flight on July 4, 1982. By this time *Challenger*, America's second shuttle, was ready for testing. Its first flight was in April 1983. Sally Ride became the first American woman in space when she was part of its second flight, in June 1983. On its third mission two months later, *Challenger* carried the first black American into space, Guion (Guy) Bluford.

Because it was a historic moment, many famous blacks went to Cape Canaveral, Florida, to watch that *Challenger* launch. Comedian Bill Cosby, former basketball star Wilt Chamberlain, and Dr. James Cheek, the president of Howard University, were among them. Ronald McNair was just as proud of Guy Bluford as the others. He understood that one of the three black astronauts had to be first. He was just looking forward to the time when his turn would come.

His turn came the following year, in February 1984, when he flew as a mission specialist aboard *Challenger*. His job was to conduct seventeen different experiments, ranging from making new alloys to harnessing solar energy to pinpointing weather and agriculture predictions. He also assisted in the launching of a $75 million communications satellite from *Challenger*'s cargo bay.

When he learned that he had been selected for the *Challenger* mission, McNair decided to have some fun while he was at it. Once in orbit, he put on a black beret and dark glasses and brought out a movie clapper board, the kind on which directors record the particular scene they are filming. His name badge read "Cecil B. McNair," a takeoff on the name Cecil B. DeMille, a famous movie director and producer.

He brought his old North Carolina A&T banner with him and displayed it on one of the walls in the crew's quarters. This was to show the world how proud he was of the black college where he had studied for his undergraduate degree. Once on the shuttle, mission control back on the ground woke him up one morning by playing the school's song.

On that mission, *Challenger* orbited the earth a total of 122 times, and McNair enjoyed every orbit. He joked about being able to see his hometown of Lake City from space. He was intrigued by the weightlessness in space and decided that the biggest problem here was moving without being clumsy. He learned that sitting or lying down took so much energy that it was simpler just to keep standing when he ate or slept. Even turning a dial too hard would start him revolving in a circle.

When the mission was over, Ronald McNair had many chances to tell about his experience. He spent a week in New York making public appearances and visiting with his proud father. He addressed the Massachusetts and South Carolina legislatures. Wherever he was invited to give a speech, he asked if his hosts could also arrange for him to speak at a local public school.

It was very important for McNair to talk to young people. He wanted them to believe that they could succeed, just as he had. As he told the graduating class at the University of South Carolina that June, "You're better than good enough. You may not come from a well-to-do financial background, you may not come from an affluent social background, you may not have glided through the University of South Carolina with the greatest of ease. But if you're willing to work hard, sacrifice, and struggle, then I proclaim today that you're better than good enough."

McNair was already looking forward to his next shuttle flight. When asked about his plans for the future, he said he envisioned himself as a resident physicist on the space station for three months each year. But in July 1984 his and Cheryl's daughter, Joy, was born, and after that he started thinking about the future of his children.

He wanted very much for them to grow up in South Carolina. His wife agreed with him. They weren't ready to make an abrupt move, but they decided to explore the possibilities. Meanwhile, McNair continued to work for NASA and was pleased to learn that he had been chosen for the *Challenger* mission scheduled for late January 1986.

In December 1985, while on a visit to his hometown, McNair had a long meeting with the dean of the engineering school at the University of South Carolina. The two spoke three more times by telephone in January. They discussed McNair's joining the faculty of the university to teach physics. In McNair's mind, the upcoming shuttle flight would more than likely be his last.

The January 28, 1986, *Challenger* flight was going to be a historic one. For one thing, seven people would be aboard, the largest crew yet to fly a shuttle. For another, one of those people chosen through a special selection process would be Christa McAuliffe, an elementary school teacher from Concord, New Hampshire. The crew would also include Mission Specialists Judith Resnik and Ellison Onizuka, payload specialist Greg Jarvis, pilot Mike Smith, and commander Francis "Dick" Scobee.

On January 28, 1986, Ronald McNair's family sat in the special spectators' section at Cape Canaveral with the families of the other astronauts. At T minus six seconds on a bright and chilly morning, the shuttle's computers sent the command to two solid rocket boosters to give it the final thrust, and the orbiter's main engines ignited, rocketing the twelve-story-tall shuttle into the air. Less than a minute later, a huge fireball raced the length of the space-craft, and a giant explosion consumed the shuttle and its entire crew.

At first, no one on the ground could believe what had happened. The shuttle had vanished, leaving just a wisp of smoke. Then, as the reality of the tragedy settled in, people broke down and cried, or were numb with shock. All seven people on board *Challenger* had disappeared with the craft. Months of investigation followed, and the final conclusion was that one of the solid rocket booster seals had failed in the cold weather and allowed flames to escape. They had burned a hole in the external fuel tank, creating a leak of liquid propellant which then exploded.

There was no need to investigate the effect of the tragedy on the nation, and especially on the families of the men and women who had died. It

Ronald McNair's family thought about what he would like them to do in his memory and decided that he would want them to set up a scholarship fund. He strongly believed that other young people who were poor should have a chance to go to school and study science, just as he had. So, less than a month after the *Challenger* tragedy, the McNair family announced the formation of the Ron McNair Scholarship Fund to help as many as 150 underprivileged students study science each year.

"Ron had a lot of hopes and dreams for young people," his family explained. "We feel we would be remiss if we did not pick up the banner."

That June, the Massachusetts Institute of Technology announced that it would name its new space center after Ronald McNair.

Selected Bibliography

Books

Branch, Taylor. *Parting the Waters: America in the King Years 1954–63*. New York: Simon & Schuster, 1988.

Brown, William Wells. *The Negro in the American Rebellion*. New York: Citadel Press, 1971.

Brownmiller, Susan. *Shirley Chisholm*. New York: Doubleday & Co., Inc., 1970.

Emanuel, Myron. *Faces of Freedom*. New York: Scholastic Book Services, 1971.

Ferris, Jeri. *Arctic Explorer: The Story of Matthew Henson*. Minneapolis: Carolrhoda Books, 1989.

Forman, James. *The Making of Black Revolutionaries*. New York: Macmillan, 1972.

Haskins, James. *Fighting Shirley Chisholm*. New York: Dial Press, 1975.

————. *Profiles in Black Power.* New York: Doubleday & Co., Inc., 1972.

Haskins, Jim. *Ralph Bunche: A Most Reluctant Hero.* New York: Hawthorn Books, 1974.

————, with Kathleen Benson. *Space Challenger: The Story of Guion Bluford.* Minneapolis: Carolrhoda Books, 1984.

Henson, Matthew A. *A Black Explorer at the North Pole.* Lincoln, NB: University of Nebraska Press, 1989.

Hughes, Langston. *Famous Negro Music Makers.* New York: Dodd, Mead & Co., 1955.

Kaplan, Sidney. *The Black Presence in the Era of the American Revolution.* New York and Washington, D.C.: New York Graphic Society, Ltd., and Smithsonian Institution, 1973.

King, Mary. *Freedom Song: A Personal Story of the 1960s Civil Rights Movement.* New York: William Morrow & Co., 1987.

Malcolm X, with Alex Haley. *The Autobiography of Malcolm X.* New York: Ballantine Books, 1965.

Patterson, Charles. *Marian Anderson.* New York: Franklin Watts, Inc., 1988.

Raines, Howell. *My Soul Is Rested: Movement Days in the Deep South Remembered.* New York: Putnam, 1977.

Williams, Juan, et al. *Eyes on the Prize: America's Civil Rights Years, 1954–1965.* New York: Viking, 1987.

Articles

Becklund, Laurie, "A Lifelong Affair with Paint," *The Atlanta Constitution*, March 15, 1988, p. 38.

Berman, Avis, "Romare Bearden: 'I Paint Out of the Tradition of the Blues,'" *Art News*, December 1980, pp. 60–67.

Brenson, Michael, "Romare Bearden: Epic Emotion, Intimate Scale," *The New York Times*, March 27, 1988, p. 41.

Brondfield, Jerome, "Eddie Robinson's Game Plan for Life," *Reader's Digest*, September 1986, pp. 163–170.

Bundles, A'Lelia P., "Madam C. J. Walker — Cosmetics Tycoon," *Ms.*, July 1983, pp. 91–94.

Campbell, Mary Schmidt, "Romare Bearden: Rites and Riffs," *Art in America*, December 1981, pp. 134–141.

Cheers, Michael D., "Requiem for a Hero: Touching the Face of God," *Ebony*, May 1986, pp. 82–84.

George, Jean Craighead, review of S. Allen Counter's book *North Pole Legacy*. The review appeared in *The New York Times Book Review*, June 30, 1991, p. 33.

Hooton, Bruce Duff, "Odyssey of an Artist," *Horizon*, August 1979, pp. 16–25.

Knox, Margaret L., "Ron McNair Was Always a Dreamer," *The Atlanta Journal and Constitution*, February 1, 1986, pp. 1–A+.

Leavy, Walter, "Eddie Robinson: Football's Winningest Coach," *Ebony*, December 1985, pp. 122–128.

——— , "Eddie Robinson: Grambling's Living Legend," *Ebony*, January 1983, pp. 60–64.

Marbach, William D., et al., "The Shuttle Tragedy: What Went Wrong?" *Newsweek*, February 10, 1986, pp. 33.

Markus, Julia, "Romare Bearden's Art Goes Home Again — To Conquer," *Smithsonian*, March 1981, pp. 71–76.

Nelson, Jill, "The Fortune That Madam Built," *Essence*, June 1983, pp. 84–86.

Reilly, Rick, "Here's to You, Mr. Robinson," *Sports Illustrated*, October 14, 1985, pp. 32–39.

Sims, Lowery S., "The Unknown Romare Bearden," *Art News*, October 1986, pp. 116–120.

Telander, Rick, "He's Tracking the Bear," *Sports Illustrated*, September 1, 1983, pp. 124–130.

Tomkins, Calvin, "Profiles: Putting Something Over Something Else," *The New Yorker*, November 28, 1977, pp. 53–57.

Wiley, Ralph, "One of Few to Hit 300," *Sports Illustrated*, October 4, 1982, pp. 67–72.

Index

Adams, John, 11–12

Advertising, Walker, Sarah (Madame C. J. Walker) and, 19, 20

Afro-American (newspaper), 97

Albuquerque, New Mexico, 65

Aldrin, Edwin, 193

Alvin Ailey Dance Company, 106

American Museum of Natural History, 36, 37

American Red Cross, blood transfusions and, 88, 89

American Revolution, 4, 6–13

Amherst College (Massachusetts), 82–83

Anaukaq (Inuit), 43, 44

Anderson, Alyce, 48, 49

Anderson, Anna, 46, 48, 49, 50, 55

Anderson, Ethel, 48, 49

Anderson, John, 46, 48, 49

Anderson, Marian, 45–62; birth of, 46–47; career of, 52–55, 61–62; church choir and, 48–49, 50; critical reviews of, 53, 54, 56, 59; education of, 50; European tour of, 55–58; honors of, 62; Lincoln Monument concert of, 45–46, 60–61; marriage of, 61; musical education of, 49, 50, 51–52, 54; racism and, 45–46, 51, 52, 59–61

Andrew (slave), 8, 10

Anthony, Susan B., 152

Apollo Theatre (Harlem, New York City), 100

Armstrong, Neil, 193

Art Students League (New York City), Bearden, Romare and, 98

Athletics: Bearden, Romare and, 96, 97; Drew, Charles R. and, 80, 82–83, 84; McNair, Ronald and, 187; Robinson, Eddie and, 124, 126, 127–130

Attucks, Crispus, 1, 3–13, 26; American Revolution and, 11–12; Boston Massacre and, 8–11; career of, 6; honors of, 13; parents of, 4; runaway slave advertisement for, 3

Attucks, John, 4

Baldwin, James, 101

Baltimore, Maryland, 27, 30

Barbados, West Indies, 147–148

Bartlett (sea captain), 38, 41, 42

Baseball, Robinson, Eddie and, 129

Basketball, Robinson, Eddie and, 129

Bearden, Bessye J., 92, 100

About the Author

JIM HASKINS is a professor of English at the University of Florida at Gainesville, and lives in New York City and Gainesville, Florida. He is the author of over eighty nonfiction books for young readers including *Black Dance in America: A History Through Its People*, which is a Coretta Scott King Award Honor Book for Nonfiction; *Black Music in America*, which won the Carter G. Woodson Award; and *Scott Joplin: The Man Who Made Ragtime*, winner of the ASCAP Deems Taylor Award. He also wrote *Get on Board: The Story of the Underground Railroad*; *Christopher Columbus: Admiral of the Ocean Sea*; *The Day Martin Luther King, Jr., Was Shot*; and *Colin Powell*.